Team Spirit

If you are responsible in any way for the quality and purpose of team gatherings, then this book is for you. Filled with inspiration as well as practical tools to deliver consistently excellent team gatherings, *Team Spirit* offers insights from a master facilitator who has enormous experience bringing out the best in others in a group setting. Can't recommend this book enough!

- Christopher Miller, Personal Development Coach for
Business Owners, christophermiller.co.nz

When people are united in a common goal, the outcome can be amazing. Unlock the collaborative power of teamwork with Antonia's expert guidance. Packed with practical tools and techniques, *Team Spirit* is your recipe for success!

- Paul Ramsay, Director, Equinox Limited

What a great book! It has redefined what I need to do as a leader and how to build teams over time through meetings. Meetings, formal and informal are the glue for our teams. Antonia shows us how to manage that interaction to build a great team and really make the difference for the people in it and then the organisation. The rhythms section helped me understand how I need to manage the flow of what my team does over time. I'd recommend this book to any leader, change practitioner or facilitator of meetings - if you're new to it or a seasoned practitioner. I've been leading teams for many years and this book is like a breath of fresh air. I soaked up everything in it and it will define how I take my team forward to meet the challenges of the next few years.

- Grant Fletcher, Head of Regional Transport, Greater Wellington Regional Council

Antonia's collection of accessible activities and tips is a fabulous source for inspiration and thorough preparation for meetings or workshops. Her approach makes the work feel effortless, natural, and enjoyable. This is an invaluable resource for any manager or facilitator looking to enrich their toolkit.

- Alice Feng, Consultant, Boston Consulting Group

Antonia worked with me to understand our context, needs and aspirations and then developed a workshop that was fit for our purpose and budget. Antonia has great energy and experience working with diverse groups of people. She had us all feeling comfortable, energised, and open to engage within minutes of starting the workshop! I would highly recommend Antonia to any team.

- Linn Araboglos, CEO, Wellington Community Trust

Antonia's framework for successful gatherings is gold! I've had the privilege of her facilitation of our team gatherings; and then the confidence to put her robust insights and purposeful activities into practice myself. Whether your team is forming, norming or storming there is something here for you.

- Lisa Docherty, Manager, Ministry of Business, Innovation & Employment

Antonia's depth of experience and understanding has helped us facilitate our own team gatherings – with purposeful design, planning and delivery. We are grateful for the many tools she has shared with us, and recommend this book to every manager out there wanting to bring their team together in a meaningful way.

- Kimberly Gilmore, General Manager, Ministry of Business, Innovation & Employment

This book is a must read for any facilitator who wants to have more impact! What's different about it? It isn't a formula to follow, but more of an enabler that supports us to be authentically unique facilitators, helping us to hone our skills and continue to make the experiences we create even more intentional and purposeful. If there is one book you invest in this year, may it be this one!

- Sarah Cretegny, Strengths Coach and Facilitator of Extraordinarily Unique Individuals and Teams, www.coachyourwild.com

Antonia is a fantastic facilitator and really gets the best out of everyone. After her workshops, I've felt energised, she really helps get into what we want as a group and leads in an upbeat manner that gives the right energy.

- Freya Lockyer, Business Advisor, Ministry of Business, Innovation & Employment

We left Antonia's workshop feeling very inspired and empowered. She brought so much wisdom and insight to how we can use our strengths to improve our work and our lives.

- Christine Langdon, Co-founder and Chief of Good, The Good Registry

When I was looking for one-to-one coaching, it was a no-brainer to ask Antonia, and she's been an asset to me as I figure out the next steps in my career. I know that I'll be using this resource to help guide my own practice.

- Ellie, Communication and Engagement Professional

TEAM SPIRIT

THE POWER OF PURPOSEFUL GATHERINGS

ANTONIA MILKOP

First published in 2024 by Hambone Publishing
Melbourne, Australia

Editing by Mish Phillips, Lexi Wight, Laura McCall, Lisa Docherty, Ashley Milkop, and Paul Ramsay
Typesetting and design by David W. Edelstein

ISBN 978-1-922357-68-7 (paperback)
ISBN 978-1-922357-69-4 (eBook)

Contents

SECTION 1

Introduction

Introduction

WHY I WROTE THIS BOOK

If whatever you do helps just one person,
you've done something wonderful.

- Blake Mycoskie, Start Something That Matters

And what if that one person goes on to have an impact on a hundred others?

That's the philosophy of this book. For every person who reads this book, you'll come away with ways to improve how you design and deliver your own team gatherings. As a result, you'll be a more effective leader and facilitator. Not only will this benefit you, but it'll also have a positive impact on all of the people who attend gatherings that you organise.

My aim is that this book provides you with useful, pragmatic, and simple tools to discover, design, and deliver better ways to bring your team together. Knowledge shared is knowledge multiplied.

It's these touchpoints of time you have with the people you work with that are at the heart of how you connect as a team. Over the years I've facilitated many meetings, workshops, team events, or away days – all of which I'll put under the umbrella of 'team gatherings'. In doing so, I've accumulated templates, resources, guides, and handy tips and tricks that will help others run successful team gatherings themselves.

I've been running a coaching and facilitation practice for several years now, and managers in organisations bring me in to facilitate their team gatherings. This is one of my favourite things to do, so I want to share that joy and the wisdom I have learned over the years with you. Most of the workshops I've facilitated for teams have been designed from scratch, based on a client's particular needs at the time. I have been able to determine, through trial and error, research, and expertise, what works well and what doesn't.

May this book make a difference to you! Grab the ideas from this book and start leading more purposeful team gatherings yourself. You will become the kind of leader that great people want to work with because you gather your people well. All the participants at your team gatherings will not only have reaped the results from a more effective way of doing things, but they'll also be inspired to run better gatherings themselves.

WHO THIS BOOK IS FOR

Whoever you are, whether you're a manager, leader, or facilitator, the concepts in this book will help you:

purpose	Keep the purpose in mind for your gatherings and know what outcomes you want to achieve.
planning	Design team gatherings well with less faff and more impact.
presence	Understand how to best 'tune in' to participants and harness energy within groups of people you work with.

You're a manager of a team

Maybe you are responsible for leading a team. You want to inspire your team. You may be under the pump getting work done, and there just aren't enough hours in the week to do all that the team needs from you. You know (in theory and from previous experience) that it's important for teams to spend time together, but you may not have the mental bandwidth to figure out how to make regular gatherings work well for your team.

The risks of not intentionally organising your time together mean you become more disconnected over time, miscommunication starts happening and even duplication of work, as people aren't communicating effectively with one another. Teams who don't spend any time together tend to have employees who are more disengaged, less productive, and less efficient. Even if you are already functioning very well together as a team, it's still important to factor in intentional team gatherings as part of sustaining a healthy and high-performing team. You don't want to risk slipping into 'complacency mode' or an 'it goes without saying' mindset in your team. Complacency hinders progress, can cause us to slip into bad habits, stifles personal growth, and cultivates a mindset of settling for good instead of going for great.

In the current climate, many organisations are cutting their budgets for things like team away days. The organisation you work for may not have the budget to hire an external facilitator to organise and orchestrate these sessions. Yet you know that you should be spending time together as a team in a regular way to make sure you don't get 'off purpose' or become disconnected in your team's mission. The months will whizz past, and nothing is going to happen unless you make it, so – as the leader of a team – the responsibility is on you! You need some quick and easy ways to help you plan, design, and deliver your team gatherings.

This book will provide you with a framework to think about your team gatherings and build courage to try out new things you learn about here and experiment with them.

This book is for you.

> *Antonia's framework for successful gatherings is gold! I've had the privilege of her facilitation of our team gatherings; and then the confidence to put her robust insights and purposeful activities into practice myself. Whether your team is forming, norming or storming there is something here for you.*
>
> - Lisa Docherty, Manager, Ministry of Business, Innovation & Employment

You're a facilitator (who wants to add to their toolkit)

You might be someone who facilitates team gatherings and are seeking some practical ideas and inspiration for work that you're doing with teams. You may want to add to your toolbox of great facilitation techniques. There are ideas shared in this book that will enable you to design and facilitate team gatherings across the various contexts you may work in. There are some easy-to-follow 'Cookie Cutters' (Section 3) to draw from, and practical ideas on how to achieve a range of outcomes within the minimum amount of time allowed (without it feeling crammed!).

Sometimes it's challenging being 'on the outside' of a team. You're not in the day-to-day existence of a team-in-action. What are some questions you ask managers you work with upfront to get a true gauge of where their team is at, and what they most need? How do you tune your efforts as a facilitator to make sure you're bringing out the best in people, getting everyone engaged, included, and involved?

I've found many of the teams I work with tend to be a lot more 'time-poor' than they used to be. It's challenging to get everyone in the office or on-site at the same time (think modern workplaces and flexible work). Team rhythms aren't necessarily the same as they used to be – we must be more intentional in how we enable teams to create connection points in the form of intentional gatherings (not necessarily always in-person).

With an increase in hybrid working (i.e., a mix of remote and on-site), teams you work with may be struggling with identifying when and how they can gather as a team – they are never all in the office or in the same place on the same day. As a facilitator, you can help these teams create some intentional rhythms that work well for everyone – with purpose, on purpose, and for purpose.

The world also seems to be experiencing a 'busyness epidemic' across our current working environments and cultures, where productivity, delivery, and outputs are given more emphasis and focus. Clients you work with may be asking you to cover a topic in two hours, which would normally take you two full days to deliver ("we just don't have enough time to spend two whole days on this" is common to hear). How can you best design the time that you're facilitating groups to ensure you meet clients where they're at, and yet make sure the outcomes everyone wants are met (without just skimming the surface)? How can you facilitate in a way that enables teams to become high-performing and highly engaged?

This book is for you.

If you are responsible in any way for the quality and purpose of team gatherings, then this book is for you. Filled with inspiration as well as practical tools to deliver consistently excellent team gatherings, Team Spirit *offers insights from a master facilitator who has enormous experience bringing out the best in others in a group setting. Can't recommend this book enough!*

- Christopher Miller, Personal Development Coach for
Business Owners, christophermiller.co.nz

WHAT IS A TEAM GATHERING?

> *Meetings can be a bit like head lice in the working-world.*
> *You can try and get rid of them,*
> *but you can never successfully eradicate them.*

You'll notice, by the way, that I rarely use the term *meetings*. I don't know about you, but I find the M-word conjures up too many negative connotations. People are often complaining about meetings – they have too many, they're too long, they're not relevant, or they spend a lot of energy trying to figure out ways to get out of them.

> *Meetings should be like salt - a spice sprinkled carefully to enhance a*
> *dish, not poured recklessly over every forkful. Too much salt destroys*
> *a dish. Too many meetings destroy morale and motivation.*
>
> - Jason Fried

A recurring pain point that I hear from managers is "I have too many meetings," or "All my time is spent in meetings, I can't actually get any work done" This problem comes up time and time again in my interactions with clients. It's not always easy to reduce the volume of them, but we can re-think how we design and deliver them.

You say meeting, I say gathering

> *You like potato and I like potahto*
> *You like tomato and I like tomahto*
> *Potato, potahto, Tomato, tomahto*
> *Let's call the whole thing off*
>
> - Ella Fitzgerald & Louis Armstrong, *Let's Call the Whole Thing Off*

There's so much more to the term 'gathering'. I was inspired by Priya Parker's book *The Art of Gathering*[1], which I read a few years ago. It helped me to think differently about how I was going about bringing teams together in a work context. I started using the term 'gathering' a lot in my own language. Instead of going to a team meeting, I'd be going to a team gathering. Instead of facilitating a team workshop, I'm facilitating a team gathering. The slight reframing, or shift of language, has not only changed my own expectations but that of others as well. People seem to look forward to a team gathering far more than attending yet-another-team-meeting.

You may question whether a gathering or a meeting is just the same thing? Isn't it just a change in semantics?! Maybe. But semantics bring important nuance to the way we communicate, listen, and understand intent.

**The term 'gathering' is people-centred,
whereas 'meeting' has a more task-centred sentiment.**

Using the expression 'team gathering' helps set the tone and intention – that people are at the centre of what you're going to accomplish when you come together.

The term 'gathering', with a purpose or theme associated with it, can have a similar affect in how it engages people and their anticipation for participation. Compare how you feel about being invited to a 'weekly team meeting' versus a 'team gathering to check in, connect, and collaborate'.

I use the following definitions throughout this book:

- A team is a group of people who work closely together and are wrapped around a common purpose or goal.
- A team gathering is when three or more people within a team

come together (in-person or online) for a specific purpose or intended result.

Team gatherings can come in many forms and flavours. There are distinctive cultural differences around the terminology and language for how people refer to their different types of team gatherings. I am most familiar with facilitating team gatherings in a New Zealand context, which we also refer to as **hui** (a Māori word which can be literally translated to mean 'cause for a gathering'[2]). I believe that many of the terms I use throughout this book can be applied cross-culturally.

Team gatherings can come in the form of information, knowledge sharing, decision making, governance, planning, team building, and social connections. Some examples of team gatherings might include:

- Workshops
- Team meetings
- Training sessions
- Away days
- Off-sites
- Information-sharing sessions
- Strategic planning sessions
- Retrospectives/reflections
- Team building
- Chew sessions
- Decision-making meetings
- Brown bag or learning sessions
- Idea generation workshops

In terms of size and scale, I refer to small team gatherings as being less than 10 people, medium as 11-30 people, and large as 30+ people. Team gatherings can be in-person, virtual, or hybrid (there's a separate chapter on that later).

Just because I'm changing a word from 'meetings' to 'gatherings' doesn't mean the existing pain points we currently have associated with meetings will vanish. Instead, I am hoping that the reframe in language will help us think differently and more creatively about how we do bring our teams together for *intentional* times – so that these times are more efficient, effective, and valuable for all those involved.

Why do we need team gatherings?

Based on the literature I've read and research I've gathered, the experiences I've had, and thinking I've done, I've identified seven reasons why all teams should gather regularly:

Teams who spend more time together are more engaged, happier, healthier, more productive, and produce better outcomes in their work, because:

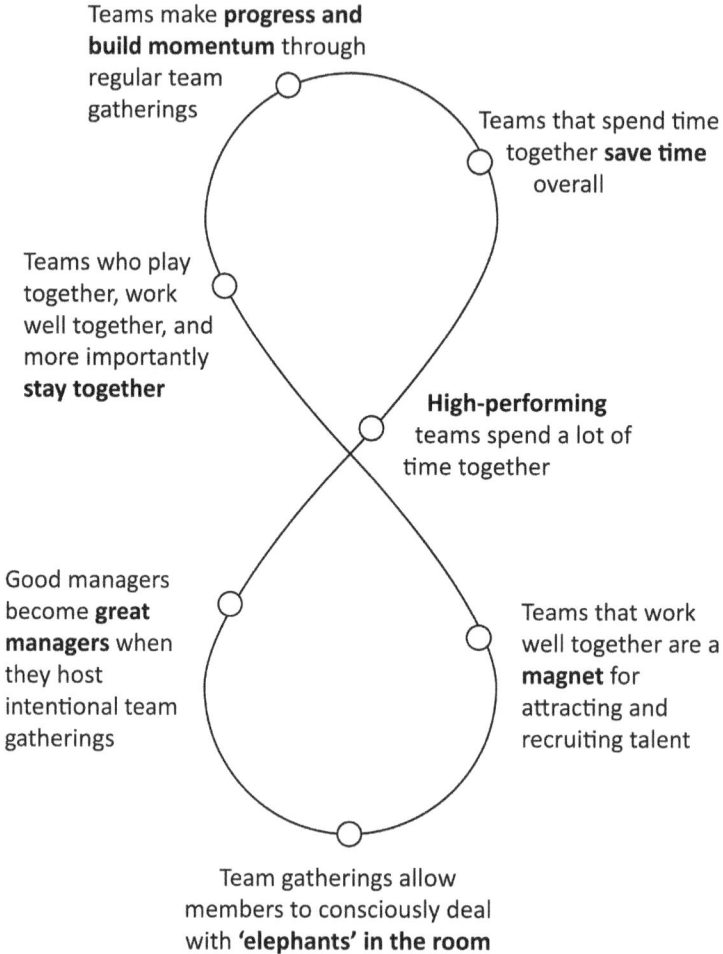

Teams make **progress and build momentum** through regular team gatherings

Teams that spend time together **save time** overall

Teams who play together, work well together, and more importantly **stay together**

High-performing teams spend a lot of time together

Good managers become **great managers** when they host intentional team gatherings

Teams that work well together are a **magnet** for attracting and recruiting talent

Team gatherings allow members to consciously deal with **'elephants' in the room**

GETTING THE MOST OUT OF THIS BOOK

Facilitating purposeful team gatherings requires a bit of artistic licence as well as some crafty tools.

The content in this book provides you with lots of 'the craft' – tools, models, tips, and tricks for designing purposeful team gatherings.

'The art' relates to your uniqueness and the style that you personally bring to applying the tools and putting them into practice. I like to think of it as the love that goes into cooking and serving a meal – it's the reason why that special recipe of Grandma's for Spaghetti Bolognese tastes so much more delicious when she cooks it compared to when anyone else tries to replicate the same recipe.

While I touch on some of the art required to run purposeful team gatherings in this book, it's up to you to discover and embrace your own authentic style – the way in which *you* facilitate gatherings for others. You bring your own unique set of skills, experiences, strengths, ideas, insights, and energy to others – own this! I encourage you to get to know your style and build your own self-awareness by discovering your strengths is a great starting point. What value do your strengths bring to the world around you? What do you need to ensure you're delivering at your best? The more you lean into your strengths the more fulfilled you are going to feel, and the more value the teams that you host gatherings for will get from you.

There are numerous assessments publicly available, which help you discover your own strengths and working style. One of my personal favourites is Gallup's CliftonStrengths® tool[3] – an incredibly useful framework, or language, which helps you not only discover your own natural talents, but how to apply these in your day-to-day work and life. It's also a helpful tool to use collectively in a team to discover how to get the best out of everyone's natural talents and lean into the dominant strengths of the team to figure out how best to gather your team[4].

The layout of sections in this book

Section 2 outlines the essential P³ ingredients to hosting successful team gatherings, why these are important and how to include them:

- **Purpose**: Help participants understand why you want them there.
- **Planning**: Design your time together well.
- **Presence**: Meet people where they're at (harness the energy).

Section 3 has a collection of easy-to-follow 'Cookie Cutters' on a variety of topics, to help you run purposeful team gatherings on your own. My objective is that the readers of this book will feel a bit like I do when following instructions in a great cookbook. You'll be able to follow some clear instructions and prompts, equipping you to facilitate really great team gatherings, yet also inject your own creative adaptations into the mix. The Cookie Cutter topics provide some examples to inspire you to create your own versions and adapt these topics as you see fit and run with them in your own teams – within your own context and timeframes, and experiment with adding and adjusting things as you see fit (following the core principles around purpose, planning, and presence – outlined in Section 2).

Section 4 reflects on what we've discovered throughout the book, how to get in touch, and outlines the range of services I provide if you want additional support.

I hope you have fun discovering the practical insights from this book and have a go experimenting with what you learn in how you facilitate your own team gatherings.

Team Spirit is all about creating purposeful moments and connection within teams, and how you gather is at the heart of that. As you implement some of the ideas in this book, I would love to hear concrete examples of what has worked and what hasn't worked for you. Please reach out!

WHAT'S WITH ALL THE COOKING METAPHORS THROUGHOUT THIS BOOK?

A happy habit of mine over weekends is to trawl through cookbooks and make a menu plan for the week for my family. I like to figure out what we've got on during the week, how much time we've got to prepare and eat, who is available to prepare or cook, and how we can balance our nutritional needs and food budget, as well as try out a few exciting new experiments along the way. We treat gathering at mealtimes as a priority in our family.

I realised a lot of these habits are mirrored in how I go about building team spirit for team events – the purpose, preparation, and planning involved. Once I started writing this book, I found more and more parallels!

I'll start by drawing on a concept to do with the benefits of family mealtimes: **families who eat together, stay together and are more resilient**. There's a huge amount of evidence-based research in the public domain about the benefits of eating together as a family. A 2022 survey by the American Health Association found that 91% of parents reported that their families were significantly less stressed when their families eat meals together regularly[5]. Some scientifically proven benefits in children also include: lower rates of depression, anxiety, and substance abuse; encouraging healthier habits; improving self-esteem; resilience; and communication skills.

The predictable rhythm of regular mealtimes together allows a chance for conversations to happen, fosters trust and belonging as part of a family, and creates a space where there may be certain 'rules of engagement' that are to be respected (e.g., no devices at the table). Mealtimes are not the only thing that helps keep families together, but they certainly have a strong predictive impact. Despite many of us knowing about the benefits of family mealtimes together, only a third of young people in New Zealand are frequently sharing family mealtimes together[6].

Teams who spend time together work well together.

A vast amount of research supports the positive impact of regular team gatherings on variables like communication, team cohesion, productivity, problem-solving, decision-making, and employee engagement. According to a recent study by Gallup[7], teams with a higher sense of cohesion are 21% more productive than teams that are not cohesive.

Given that many of us spend a vast number of our waking hours with our work colleagues, should we not apply the same principles of family mealtimes within our teams? Instead of just functioning together as a team and doing what we're supposed to do in our work, outputs, and deliverables, what emphasis are we putting on gathering and the regular rhythm of coming together as a team? Are we making it meaningful? Food is not necessarily an essential part of it (although food is always a bonus!).

In the pages that follow, I outline the recipes and ingredients that I've learned over the years for how to bring teams of people together successfully. There are many parallels between the aspects of meal planning (time, budget, balancing nutritional needs, who's available), with the elements of designing purposeful team gatherings (time, budget, balancing participant needs and what goes on the agenda).

My hope is that this book provides practical resources that others can pick up and use for their own facilitation of team gatherings. These ideas and tools will not only make you feel more empowered, capable, and confident in running your own team gatherings, but they will also help your team become high performing as a result. Just as a good recipe combines with the flair of the chef to deliver a delicious meal, a successful team gathering requires both craft (the tools you use) as well as art (who you are as a facilitator and how you use that).

WHAT MAKES A GREAT TEAM?

Given that you are reading this book, I'm guessing that you may have already explored a lot of research and literature around what makes a great team. I'm a fan of Patrick Lencioni's work around *The Five Dysfunctions of Teams*, which explores the natural dysfunctions that teams invariably face (given that we are all human and imperfect), and highlights the crucial, yet difficult, task of identifying what makes great teamwork. The book explores the common dysfunctions that teams face, and the variables that make healthy, high-performing teams. *Spending time together* is one of the essential ingredients.

> *Great teams spend a lot of time together,*
> *which results in them saving time.*
>
> - Patrick Lencioni, The Five Dysfunctions of Teams

Can you think back over your career to date, and reflect on teams that you've been a part of where you felt you were making a useful contribution, were engaged, connected with your colleagues, and felt part of something bigger? What were the essential elements for you?

. . . .

. . . .

. . . .

. . . .

Given that I'm writing a book about team gatherings, it seems appropriate to say what I think makes a great team. There's a wealth of inspiring content in books I've previously read noted in the references for you, and I've summarised below some essential ingredients that I think make for a great team to work in. Everyone is different, but in my opinion, the best teams I've worked with over the 25 odd years of my working life are teams that:

- Are highly engaged in their purpose as a team and the purpose and mission of the organisation they work in.
- Have a manager or leader who is authentic and knows how to lead people (building trust, stability, compassion, and hope in their team members)[8].
- Know how to connect, communicate, and collaborate.
- Have a high-trust environment (people aren't scared of conflict and know how to agree and disagree constructively together) – they've also got each other's backs when things go wrong.
- Get a lot of stuff done (but don't burn out) – and the things they're doing are focussed on impact not just 'outputs for delivery's sake'.
- Have individuals in them who have high levels of self-awareness and an appreciation of others in the team and know how to rely on one another and their strengths to work together.
- Nurture people to grow and flourish (both within and/or outside the team).
- Know how to celebrate success.

The best teams I've worked in have always had regular team gatherings for different purposes, with healthy rhythms and routines. The team gatherings have been the oxygen, the topics the fuel, and the people the heat. Regular team gatherings keep a team alive and firing on all cylinders. Purposeful team gatherings don't just happen by chance – they're like the muscles of a team that need regular exercise to keep a healthy heartbeat going.

Great teams are people magnets – other people want to connect, work with, help, and engage with them. There's something quite remarkable about working in a great team. I love the strengths-based approach to building a team, as it doesn't expect everyone to excel at everything – more importantly, it's expecting everyone to discover and become aware of their own strengths, as well as weaknesses, and rely on one other collectively to achieve great things.

A strengths-based team is an interdependent group of imperfect but talented contributors valued for their strengths, who need one another to realise individual and team excellence.

- Gallup

Building a high-performing team takes great design, purpose, and vision as well as authentic leadership. We are all human, but how we harness our humanness in leadership is the essence of authentic leadership at its best.

Team gatherings are one of the essential ways in which teams connect, share, and collaborate. High performing teams have healthy habits, and one of these is having regular touch points for connection and coordination.

REFRAMING COMMON MYTHS FOR MANAGERS

You've probably had good and bad experiences of team gatherings. Over my working life, mostly in the UK and New Zealand, I've taken part in a lot of different types of team gatherings. Some have been great, but, unfortunately, I've often experienced gatherings that are poorly organised, purposeless, badly delivered and are inefficient, ineffective, and a waste of everyone's time. It's frustrating and I wish it didn't have to happen so often. *What is the point? What's in it for me? Why are we here? What are we trying to achieve by bringing all these people together?* You get a lot more out of a team if they know what's coming up and the purpose of why they are coming together.

> **Myth#1:** Someone else will organise team gatherings for me if we need them.
>
> **Reframe:** You are the manager/leader of this team. Own your space, know that the buck starts and stops with you to make sure you plan team gatherings.

There is a lot of pressure on managers to 'do more with less', whether that's having fewer people, hours, or resources at your fingertips to get the work of your team accomplished. Some managers assume they can make their team more productive by reducing the number of touchpoints your team has together to run more efficiently, especially given that scheduling time in diaries is a pain point for many in sucking up valuable time. More than ever, managers and their teams are expected to deliver more, be more productive, perform better – but somehow end up seeing less of each other to accomplish all of this. It's almost like we're in the middle of a global delivery-epidemic. Heads down, get to work!

> **Myth #2:** We can't afford the budget for quarterly away days.
>
> **Reframe:** You don't necessarily have to spend much money on larger scale team gatherings - having regular ones means you'll save costs in the longer term.

Spending time out of the normal day-to-day activities to organise a team gathering can feel like an extravagant use of time and budget to some people, or maybe your organisation considers things like 'away days' as optional extras or nice-to-haves. In the current climate of budget cuts, financial restraint, and a high demand for work outputs with limited capacity and resources, it can be easier to either postpone or minimise time and money spent on team building, team away days, or team workshops on purposeful topics. Cutting budgets on team gatherings can often be seen as a quick win within constrained budgets or removing 'unnecessary' expenditure, they simply get trumped by other priorities.

Team days are an essential part of a team's rhythms. The science and theory behind prioritising them shows that teams become more efficient and productive as a result – saving costs in the longer run.

Myth#3: We can't find the time to all get together.

Reframe: There is plenty of time (if you plan ahead of time). The key is to focus the time you have. Direct your attention towards longer term outcomes. Gatherings that have no purpose or intended result are a waste of time. Don't get rid of your team gatherings. Instead, treat them as a priority, schedule them, and figure out a way to plan or design them better.

The global pandemic of 2020-2022 shone a spotlight on many teams and organisations as people found that their traditional ways of working weren't actually working that well. Existing team gatherings became virtual or hybrid ones, and unless they were designed well (i.e. adapted in their design for purpose, presence, and intended outcomes), they were at best disengaging and at worst a flop! One of the benefits, or consequences, of moving to virtual during the pandemic was shining a light on the importance of designing team gatherings well.

With increasingly flexible workplaces, competing modes of connection via technology, and the human habit of 'always being switched on' it's no wonder we can sometimes feel a bit desperate about the possibility of finding time and space to bring our team together and whether they can make it on the same date. It's not necessarily straightforward arranging suitable times and spaces where people who work together can come together. Yet we know it's important to do so. It's worth planning well in advance.

Myth #4: To have meaningful team gatherings, we need to all be there physically in-person.

Reframe: Meaningful connections can extend beyond in-person interactions. Create touchpoints for connection and purpose, even if these are virtual or hybrid ones. It'll make a huge difference.

I've met many leaders who struggle to connect virtually with their colleagues. They are happy to wait until 'the time is right' for people to all come together in-person. What most of these leaders find is that it's nearly impossible to gather their people together in-person at the same time. It takes a huge amount of logistical effort to do so. If you can't gather easily in-person on a regular basis, you will benefit from designing purposeful touchpoints and connections (virtually) with intended purpose and results, rather than just waiting until you can next meet in-person.

Do any of these myths ring true for you? How so?

. . . .

. . . .

. . . .

. . . .

Story - The leader who kept postponing their team gatherings

I worked with a client who was choosing to postpone the away days they had planned throughout the year for their leadership team. They kept scheduling them, then cancelling them at the last minute, as they weren't able to all come together in-person. Over the course of an entire year, this team still hadn't managed to all gather together to talk about some of the essential things they needed to cover, over and above their transactional day-to-day activities. There was always a valid excuse (people were too busy, or they preferred to gather in-person). They instead chose to focus on the transactional day-to-day priorities when they gathered (which of course were important as well), but this all came at a cost to the overall cohesion as a team. Days, weeks, and months went by, and I observed that trust between the individuals in this team was eroding and that they were feeling less engaged. Team members were becoming more defensive and sceptical; they were getting frustrated with each other and they were losing their ability to focus on the longer-term goals for the organisation.

Given all the benefits of intentionally gathering as teams, it should come as no surprise that members of teams that don't gather regularly have individuals in them who are likely to feel more disconnected from the rest of their colleagues, and more disengaged about their work and overall job satisfaction.

Story – the leader who committed to regular team gatherings

On the other hand, I can share a story about another client I worked with who understood the importance of having team gatherings as an essential part of the healthy functioning of the whole group. This leader had originally intended to run quarterly in-person away days for her group as a way of coming together to connect, and cover some of the training, topics, and challenges that the group was facing over the course of the year. Despite consistent setbacks and logistical hiccups (add a global pandemic into the mix, lockdowns, legislative changes, and a geographically-dispersed team), this leader instead committed to rearranging these full-day away days into regular virtual team gatherings in smaller, bite-sized pieces (covering topics discretely that had been originally intended as full-day experiences). As a consequence, this group of 40 individuals were far more connected throughout the course of the year despite all the setbacks they experienced.

The effort and focus on team cohesion and collaboration was evidenced in their increased engagement survey results at the end of the year. It was a marvellous thing to be able to witness the deeper connection these people had together, and their ability to straddle conflict as it arose in a high-trust (mostly virtual) environment together, covering with grace and ease some very tricky stuff. I think a lot of the success of this group boils down to the fact that they intentionally gathered on a regular basis over the course of the year – nothing was going to stop them.

SECTION 2

The 3 Ps:
Purpose, Planning, Presence

It's All in P³

Coming together is a beginning, staying together is progress,
and working together is success.

- Henry Ford

T he secret sauce to make any team gathering a success is in the essential ingredients, P³ (P to the power of 3). This section explains
why you might need any one of these things, and why it makes a
magnitude of difference when you think about all three.

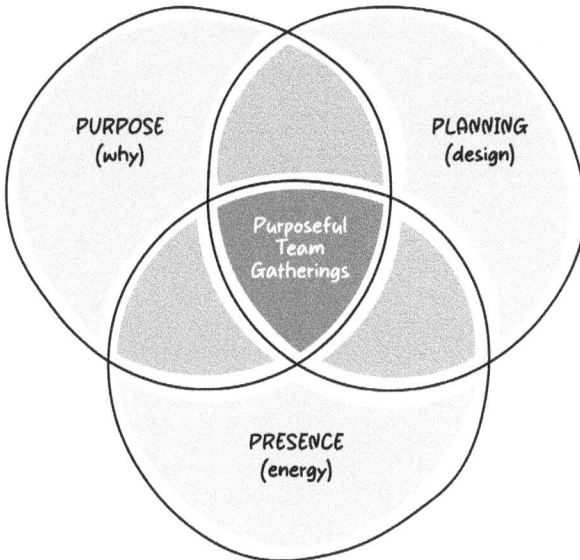

THE 3 Ps

Purpose

Why are we gathering? What do we want to achieve? Your team gatherings need a purpose. If you don't know *why* you want to gather, your time together is likely to be vague and fruitless. Every time you bring a group of people together, it's important to know and be clear on *why* you're coming together, and make sure you share this purpose with all participants.

> *Time spent together without purpose is meaningless.*

Knowing what you want to cook up beforehand (whether it's a 15 minute quick fix, grabbing a takeaway, or creating something more elaborate), helps you set the scene for what to expect and how participants in will show up to your gathering.

Planning

Great team gatherings don't just happen by chance. Hosting purposeful team gatherings requires some intentional design. This can take many forms, but it will be the process that's going to blend your time together in a way that helps you achieve the outcomes you want. Planning includes considering what you need to think about beforehand, during, and after your gathering: practical considerations that you need to take into account; likely risks or obstacles that might crop up and how you plan to deal with these.

Good design is making something intelligible and memorable.
Great design is making something memorable and meaningful.
- Dieter Rams

Good design beforehand saves time and leads to better results. Just as a good recipe produces a delicious meal, a well-designed plan means you're less likely to burn your end results, miss something, or add salt to the mix when you meant to add sugar.

Presence

Presence describes the 'people energy' in your team gathering – both the energy of the participants and that of the facilitator, and anyone else involved. People's presence makes a difference – every individual in a gathering contributes to the overall vibe of that gathering – even if their own role is being a passive participant.

The success of your gathering relies on appropriately harnessing the people-energy in the room – how can you bring out the best in the participants so that they feel motivated and engaged in the purpose and create traction to produce results?

Understand your audience, but never overlook your position within it.

Different types of food give us different nutritional needs – learning how to balance out the right amounts of all the elements is a recipe for success.

WHY YOU NEED ALL THREE (PXPXP = P³)

Goldilocks knew what 'just right' tasted like.
You want to make sure you don't overcook or undercook
your meal; but add just the right amount of Purpose,
Planning, and Presence to create a great gathering.
Too much or too little of any one ingredient may spoil the mix.

What happens when a team gathering only takes into account one or two of the three essential ingredients: Purpose, Planning, and Presence?

As a host of any team gathering, make sure you are alert to which of the three Ps may not be getting enough weight in the way you organise and design your gathering. We'll look at this in more detail in the coming chapters.

You'll find that:

- *Without purpose* - your planning will be time-consuming and probably miss the mark.
- *Without planning* - you risk not covering all that you need to in the time that you have or be able to prepare for unforeseen eventualities, which are likely to happen!
- *Without presence* - you're missing the connection between yourself and who's participating and making sure you engage with why they are there.

Do you know why you are organising this gathering?

. . . .

. . . .

Do you know what you need to cover in this gathering?

. . . .

. . . .

Do you know what each of the participants needs from this gathering?

. . . .

. . . .

Perhaps everyone knows *why* they are there and what they aim to get out of their time together (Purpose). The whole thing has been beautifully designed and organised (Planning). However, little attention has been given to the audience attending or managing the energy in the room during the day (Presence).

There may be some team gatherings that are meticulously planned, with a clear and packed agenda prepared beforehand. But the 'why' is completely missing. I've been to many meetings like this in the past. The group has a thoroughly interesting conversation – but no traction or action comes from it.

Let's talk about the intersections between each of the three Ps:

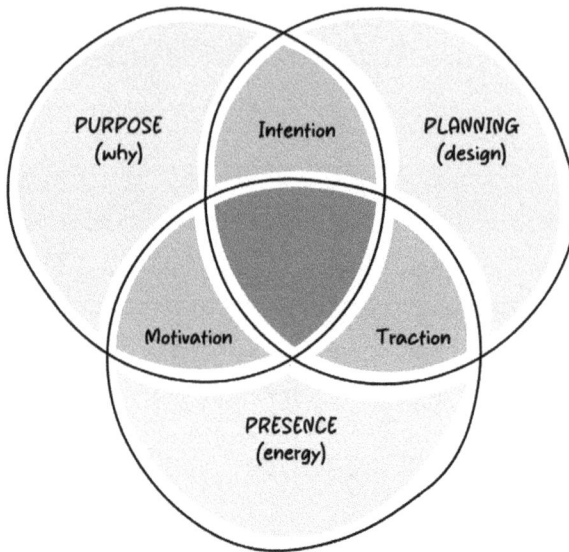

- **Purpose + Planning** creates ***intention***. Participants know why they're turning up and what's expected of them and others.
- **Planning + Presence** creates ***traction***. Participants are engaged and willing to participate and make stuff happen – before, during, and after the gathering.
- **Presence + Purpose** creates ***motivation***. People know why they're there and how they're showing up. They are inspired to take part.

Here's what happens when one or more of the essential ingredients within the 3Ps is missing.

PURPOSE (why)	WITH	WITHOUT
	Meaningful	Vague
	Intentional	Distracting
	Easy and straight-forward	Difficult and confusing
	Engaging	Passive
	Focussed	Scattered

PLANNING (what + when)	WITH	WITHOUT
	Time well spent (efficient)	Poorly time-managed and lack of flow
	Covered intentions and captured purpose and outcomes (effective)	Vague and pointless, not engaging
	Organised, yet flexible	Disorganised, or rigid
	Team is seen as a whole system	Team is seen as individual parts, not a whole
	Pleasant surprises, including intentionally created ones	Unpleasant surprises (e.g., venue double booked, tech didn't work, uninvited people turn up, or those that were supposed to come got double booked!)

PRESENCE (who + how)	WITH	WITHOUT
	Intuitive	Rigid
	Meets needs of participants where they are	Off-point for participants or doesn't meet needs or the outcomes desired
	Role clarity	Roles are unclear
	Traction, energy, and motivation from participants	Lack of traction, unmotivated and not harnessing the people energy in the room
	Safe space to contribute	Unsafe
	People bring their authentic selves	People don't bring their best selves

Can you reflect back on a team gathering you've recently been to where something was missing? Can you describe what was missing?

. . . .

. . . .

. . . .

. . . .

The next three chapters cover the essential ingredients in all three Ps. We will explore why all three are important and how to ensure you have all the ingredients for each.

Purpose

(Know your why)

If you don't know your 'why', you'll have no idea what direction you're going in. It's a bit like having some flour, sugar, salt, and butter, but not a clue about what you're going to make with these ingredients. There are certainly a lot of possibilities!

WHY PURPOSE MATTERS

I meet a lot of teams who have a regular 'team meeting' scheduled in their diaries, but these meetings can lack any real purpose behind them other than 'we probably should regularly catch up as a team'.

Given the lack of articulated purpose, the process can drift into something like each individual contributing to a round-table on what they are working on at the moment (yawn). Depending on the numbers in the team, this can take a while (even though people are perhaps told they have only a couple of minutes each).

These team gatherings need to explain *why* they're coming together – is it for connection? Is it to ensure they are avoiding duplication of work? Is it to help each other with issues or challenges cropping up? Is it to share information or resources that might be useful for their colleagues? Or is it a competition on who's got the longest task list? (I'm hoping it's not the latter, yet that's how these types of gatherings tend to turn out if there's no communication about a clear purpose).

> *If you're not clear with why you want to gather,*
> *your team won't know why they're there.*

A courageous experiment for you to try

Try this experiment for when you next receive a calendar invite for a gathering: if the sender hasn't articulated what the purpose is, tell them you intend to decline unless they communicate what the purpose is.

I've tested this assumption above with managers who are complaining about the sheer volume of meetings they have in their calendars. I propose that they try experimenting with only accepting calendar invites where a clear purpose has been articulated, and an explanation given of why they specifically need to be there.

By doing this, it shifts the way we host our own gatherings – what do we include in, say, the calendar invite that gets sent out? How do we share the purpose behind why we're gathering, and what expectations (spoken and unspoken) do we have of the roles we want people to play when they come along?

In the past, I've seen whole days scheduled in people's diaries with a subject line like 'Branch Away Day', and yet there's no purpose shared with the group about why they are taking this whole day out of normal, day-to-day work.

As well as your team *knowing* the purpose of the gathering, it's also important for them to know the purpose *in advance*. This helps set the intention of your gathering and plants the seeds of purpose so that the team can anticipate, prepare, and bring their best selves.

Don't leave the purpose until the last minute. Think of it like pre-heating the oven to the correct temperature before you put your dish in to cook.

Always share <u>why</u> you're gathering. It's important to share this intention ahead of time and to share it with all participants.

A purposeful gathering, by contrast, is one that will feel vital, people will be keen to take part and know why they've been asked to attend. Their mindset will be prepared for how they want to show up and what they would like to contribute to this time together.

OUTCOMES FIRST

Begin with the ~~end~~ experience in mind.

- adapted from Steven Covey's famous quote from *7 Habits of Highly Effective People*

Perhaps you're a manager and you know you 'should' be bringing your team together more, but you're not sure where to start. At the outset, I have found it's always good to start with the experience in mind: how do you want the team to think, feel, and behave as a result of coming together?

It's important to first understand your own intentions, then make sure you clearly articulate these to others, and manage any expectations you have as a result of bringing your team together.

How do you want the team to think, feel, and behave as a result of gathering together?

This is one of the first questions I ask of all my clients. People find it a helpful question to consider. And, as a facilitator, I find the answers hold rich content with which to design our time together well.

There's a risk if you don't ask this question upfront. You may go forth and deliver a whole set of pre-prepared materials on a particular topic which may be rich in content and value, and relevant to what the team may have originally asked you for, but you are missing out on the *real* outcomes intended. Knowing the desired outcomes enables you to tweak *what* and *how* you deliver to this particular group, based on what they *really* need.

Some examples

I have found this short, yet meaningful, question has prompted a context-rich response to help plan and design our time together in the best way possible.

Here are some examples of answers I've had from clients when I've posed this question to them:

> "We're currently quite disconnected as a team, and haven't come together in-person for over a year. I'd like to create a safe space so that my team can build trust with each other and appreciate each other's different styles and ways of working. By doing this, I hope we'll be more productive as a team and able to deal with conflict more easily."

"We're currently quite silo-ed as a team as we're spread out across different parts of the country. I'd like the team to learn how to rely on their counterparts in other parts of the country more and work together more collaboratively – we'd likely be more efficient as a result if everyone is working to their strengths."

"We've got some tricky dynamics in our team where there's an obvious lack of self-awareness about the impact some individuals are having on others because of the way they operate and things they say to others. I'd like the time we have together to first focus on building our self-awareness of our own individual strengths, and have opportunities to work together in small groups to better understand each other, our ways of working and our blind spots."

"As a group we're excellent at 'the doing' and we're always on top of knowing when things are done or not. However, there's a key difference between 'done versus won'. We seem to be addicted to the 'doing', but less observant of the resulting impacts and outcomes of our work. I'd like the team to think about what success looks like for us as a group (outside of delivering outputs on time), what winning looks like/feels like, and reflect on the past as to whether we've been as effective and efficient as we can be."

"Less 'I' more 'WE'. I want the team to come away from the day with a 'Team Voice' – currently the team look at things from an individual perspective, and seem more concerned about their individual accountability rather than group results. As a result of whatever we do at the workshop, I'd like the team to think more collectively, feel more connected, and behave in a way that puts us above me in all their work."

"We need to do an activity together that both helps us understand each other's working strengths and styles better, but also can lead into a conversation about our trust and resilience as a team (being open and honest with each other, and being able to give and receive feedback)."

"I want us to think more deeply about where we're at in our strategic planning going forward and what the next steps are. I want the team to feel they've got more skin in the game (i.e. it's not just the leadership team that decide on or put together the strategic plan). As a result of our time away together, I would like to see team members putting their hands up for getting involved in future work (without the leadership team having to ask them)."

"I want us to feel more connected, and with a generous disposition toward each other and the wider organisation; having a shared sense of purpose; feeling empowered, and that we can make a difference/make change. In a reflective mindset, I want us to be ready to take the opportunity presented to continue to know ourselves better and build on our strengths."

"I want the team to come away with a clear sense of direction for the next quarter. And what roles we all play in the various activities we're taking on."

By asking this question (and receiving an honest answer), you'll get some useful clues as to how to design and shape the day for successful delivery.

Sometimes it can be hard for a leader to articulate clearly what they want the outcomes to be. In this case, as the facilitator, make sure to probe and discover a little more about where the team is currently at – and where they ideally want to be. If the person initiating the gathering still can't answer, then you probably need to ask them again why they want to gather their team together in the first place (perhaps they've been told they need to, in which case ask for permission to talk to the person who's requested this for their team and probe *them* more deeply!).

Can you see any common threads in the examples I've shared above? I've captured some common themes I've noticed over time in these conversations I've had.

Outcomes Matrix - Think, Feel and Behave

THINK	From	To
	1 ← - →	10
	Scattered ← - - - - - - - - - - - - - - - - - →	Collective
	Shallow ← - - - - - - - - - - - - - - - - - - →	Deep
	Confused ← - - - - - - - - - - - - - - - - - →	Clear
	Problem focused ← - - - - - - - - - - - →	Possibility focused

FEEL	From	To
	1 ← - →	10
	Disengaged ← - - - - - - - - - - - - - - - →	Engaged
	Helpless ← - - - - - - - - - - - - - - - - - →	Empowered
	Fearful ← - - - - - - - - - - - - - - - - - - →	Courageous
	Closed ← - - - - - - - - - - - - - - - - - - - →	Open
	Guarded ← - - - - - - - - - - - - - - - - - →	Vulnerable

BEHAVE	From	To
	1 ← - →	10
	Muddled ← - - - - - - - - - - - - - - - - - - →	Coordinated
	Disconnected ← - - - - - - - - - - - - - - →	Connected
	Frowning ← - - - - - - - - - - - - - - - - - - →	Smiling
	Relying on leader ← - - - - - - - - - - →	Relying on others
	Passive ← - - - - - - - - - - - - - - - - - - →	Responsive
	Being asked ← - - - - - - - - - - - - - - - →	Offering
	Individual ← - - - - - - - - - - - - - - - - →	Collective

An experiment for you to try

I want you to think of an upcoming team gathering you are either leading or taking part in. Ask yourself the questions in the steps and see how easy it is to answer these questions.

If you're struggling with thinking of ideas, then imagine this scenario instead:

Scenario:

Imagine that you are a manager who is bringing your team together for a whole day next month. You haven't managed to gather in-person as a team for a whole year. You don't have any budget this year to bring in a professional facilitator to help you design, organise, or facilitate the day itself, so you've asked someone from another team to be the facilitator for the day.

You would like to involve a few of your team members to help with putting together some activities you can do during the day, as a way of making them feel more involved and connected. You are relying on the limited capacity and expertise of your team and this other team member to organise the day and facilitate it.

You've got a good idea in your own mind about where the team is currently at and what they might need during a day out of the office, but you are struggling to articulate this clearly. You want to make clear what's in your head and articulate this out loud so that you can share this with those helping organise the day so you know you're all making the most of the time you've got together as a team (and you can leave them to go forth and organise it all!).

You need to provide clear instructions to those helping with the day about what you want to get out of this team gathering. How do you want the team to think, feel, and behave as a result of the gathering?

STEP 1

Review the 'Outcomes Matrix' table above and circle some of the variables that you think matter most for your team (feel free to add your own too). Make sure to choose at least one from each section: Think, Feel, and Behave.

STEP 2

Give your team a score of 1 to 10 on each of the Think-Feel-Behave variables you have chosen on your list from Step 1. Make sure you give a short reason as to why you chose this score.

For example, if one of the outcomes you're seeking is 'Collective', but you currently think your team is very scattered or haphazard in the way they think and operate together, then you might give this a low score of around 2/10.

STEP 3

Review your scores, and decide which shifts you think are most important for your team at this stage.

Depending on your circumstances, you may even want to involve the team in this process. Don't worry about what's realistic at this stage or put any mental barriers up by thinking about achievability, just go with your gut and describe it how it is. For example, you might find yourself reviewing a low 2/10 score and thinking how amazing it would be if that variable could shift up to a 5/10. Or you may find yourself seeing a 9/10 score and thinking how important it will be to ensure you maintain this high score.

STEP 4

You'll now be able to clearly describe what the current situation is like in your team and what outcomes you hope to get out of the team gathering. Share and test this with those people that are helping you organise the team gathering.

STEP 5

Summarise your outcomes statements above into one, short and pithy purpose statement – to clearly state why you are bringing your team together.

STEP 6

Share the purpose of the gathering with the team (and preferably in the subject line of a calendar invite in their diaries!).

The outcomes matrix above isn't intended as a definitive answer to 'what you should do', but more a helpful guide so you can manage any assumptions you may have about the team's current state and where you want to get them to. Use it as a tool to help guide your thinking and conversations with the manager or team, helping to determine what the team actually needs as a result of this gathering. Use your instincts to guide you and be prepared to test or challenge your assumptions with others.

A REAL-LIFE EXAMPLE

Here's a past example of my own for a team for whom I was facilitating a gathering. I've illustrated the five steps above through my explanations below – these insights came from a short, 20-minute conversation with the manager of this team.

From our conversation together, it appeared to me that the shifts, or variables, which mattered most for this team to address at their gathering were:

- **Think**: Moving from Confused to Clear
- **Feel**: Moving from Disengaged to Engaged
- **Behave**: Moving from Relying on the leader, to Relying on others, or each other, more.

I gave them the following scores on a scale of 1-10 (with my reasons given below):

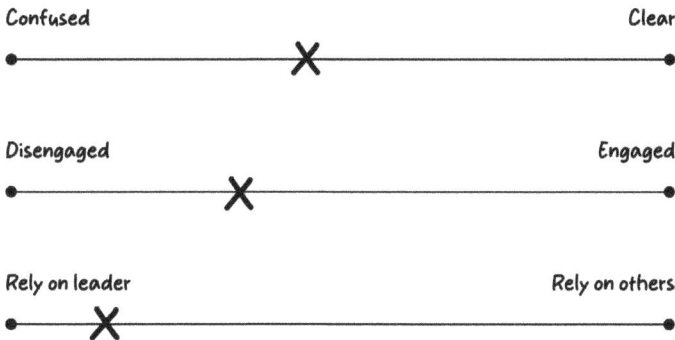

Confused   Clear
●————————————X————————————————●

Disengaged   Engaged
●—————————X—————————————————————●

Rely on leader   Rely on others
●———X———————————————————————————●

- Clarity (5/10): The team did not have a clear vision or purpose as a result of ongoing organisational restructuring. Team members were feeling confused about what parts of the work programme were important or not.

- Engaged (4/10): The manager had just gotten back the engagement survey results for her team and while the scores were quite high overall, she instinctively felt that the team was less engaged than this because of the current team morale and a decline in enthusiasm for the work over the last few months. She believed this was a result of a number of factors, including an organisational restructure that was dragging on and creating a lot of uncertainty about the future direction for the group; a lack of purpose or vision for the team's work; and the fact that the team had four different managers over the last year.
- Rely on Others (2/10): Currently all 11 of the team members were coming to the manager individually for support (for coaching, mentoring, and other support). While she genuinely wanted to be available and approachable to support her staff, the reality was that she was only in this position for another couple of months and she simply did not have the time, capacity, or capability to best support them with all their needs. How might she equip and empower the team to rely on others more for support so they were set up better for the future?

I sent a summary to the manager with my understanding of the outcomes she was seeking – to clarify whether these hit the mark or not (before I went ahead and planned for the day's activities):

- Getting clarity on the work programme and who is able to do what.
- Help individuals feel more engaged as well as connected with each other.
- Figuring out what support team members would need to enable them to thrive as individuals and equipping them with ways of gaining that support.

She immediately came back to me and said 'yes, that's exactly what we need'. We'd managed to clarify concisely what was needed for this gathering. This meant I could get right on with planning and designing – knowing I'd probably saved heaps of to-ing and fro-ing time later down the track (you may be interested to know that the whole 'scoring process' and choosing the most relevant variables took me all of 10 minutes).

By asking these questions upfront, the manager was able to think through what her team needed and articulate exactly what she wanted to get out of this gathering to her team. She then shared the purpose and intended outcomes of the team gathering with the rest of the team via a calendar invite that went out in advance – this helped the rest of the team tune in to the purpose for the day and its intentions. It also enabled them to feel motivated and look forward to being a part of something meaningful.

A distinction between outcomes versus goals

Outcomes and goals can be seen as being much of a muchness and are sometimes used interchangeably. I'd like to provide some nuance to clarify how they are different so you can indeed focus your gatherings on outcomes, not just goals.

> *Goals are what you aim to achieve,*
> *while outcomes are what happens as a result of your actions.*

When you pose the question 'what outcomes do you want to achieve from this gathering?', some people may answer you with a list of *goals* they'd like to pursue. Using the real-life example from earlier, my conversation with the manager of this team might go something like this:

Me: *What outcomes do you want from this gathering?*

Manager: *I want us to go through our work programme and timelines and figure out who's doing what.*

Notice they are referring to goals, *not* outcomes. I'd want to help steer the conversation towards what outcomes this manager was seeking using the Outcomes Matrix: how does this manager want the team to think, feel, and behave by the end of the gathering? Exploring *why* the team needs to go through the work programme and timelines may help uncover the actual outcomes required.

In the real-life example earlier, the outcomes sought were that team members have clarity over the work programme; they feel engaged and supported; and they can help identify ways to rely on one another.

Having defined your outcomes – how can you put some legs on these outcomes to result in action? And how will you know if you've been successful in achieving these things? That's where goals come in. While outcomes are tangible or intangible results that emerge from the pursuit of goals, goals are:

Specific: Clearly defined and focused.
Measurable: Quantifiable and trackable.
Achievable: Realistic and attainable.
Relevant: Aligned with overall objectives and purpose.
Time-bound: Have a specific timeframe for completion.

Taking the example from earlier, some SMART goals for the outcomes identified for this gathering were:

- Ensure that at least 30% of the gathering allows space for connections between team members, meaningful conversations, and dialogue, including Q&A with a guest speaker, or inviting a key partner who is relevant for the success of our work programme.

- Identify what can be realistically achieved over the next 3 months given our current team capacity and capability (a keep/stop/start conversation).
- Update the work programme for the next 3 months, and ensure we communicate these updates with our key stakeholders and governance group at least two weeks before the next governance meeting to manage expectations.
- Determine team members' roles and responsibilities for each of the tasks across the work programme, to increase clarity of everyone's part to play in our work programme.
- Identify what additional support we need to achieve what we need to over the next 3 months – both internally and externally.

Reflecting on our analogy of recipes for team gatherings, if the desired outcomes are to look forward to eating together, create a sense of belonging and connectedness, and spend some quality family time together, then the goals are what help get us there, i.e. writing a shopping list for specific ingredients and checking what's in season, doing the shopping, prepping and cooking the meal within a 2.5 hour window, figuring out what sequence to prepare and cook things in, having everything ready and table set before guests arrive at 6pm, finding some fun thing to add to the table settings to create a sense of belonging (ask kids to design some name tags for guests with a question on the back and decorate the table with some creative flair).

Capturing data on outcomes

How will you know if you've been successful? What can you do to measure success? See if you can try and capture any 'outcomes data' before and after your gathering. Even if it's very subjective, it'll give you some clues as to whether you're making progress.

Data can be as simple as a few questions on a numerical Likert scale (from 'strongly disagree' to 'strongly agree') – focused on questions related to the outcomes sought.

For example, you can ask all team members to give a score on a scale of 1-10 about how well they think the outcomes were met (even better if you can ask similar questions at the *beginning* and *end* of the gathering). It's helpful to make this anonymous if you can. Capturing this simple data only takes just a few minutes and it will give you a sense of whether you've hit the nail on the head in achieving the outcomes you desired, or if you perhaps need to re-group and try things a different way.

For the real-life example above, this is an example of a short survey you could run both the *beginning* and the *end* of a gathering for this team to see how you're progressing against the outcomes sought.

Score yourself 1 to 10 (from 'strongly disagree' to 'strongly agree') on the following:

____ I am clear on the work expected of me over the next quarter

____ I know who's doing what across our team's work programme

____ I know who to go to for support when I need it – both within our team and externally

____ I feel a sense of belonging in this team.

This types of quick check-in (and how the scores vary both before and after the team gathering) provides helpful insights as to how a team thinks they're tracking with the outcomes they set out to achieve.

A THEME FOR YOUR GATHERING

We have many demands for our daily attention, so to get buy-in for something it helps to have catchphrases or memorable themes people can hook on to. It's a bit like a pretty picture alongside your recipe in the cookbook – I'm far more inclined to engage with and cook recipes that have photos alongside them compared with those that don't.

Now that you are clear about why you want to bring the team together (purpose), what intended results you want (outcomes), and how you're going to get there (goals), a *theme* helps consolidate all these things into something snappy and engaging to help the team get excited and look forward to the gathering.

I have always found that having a pithy and catchy theme for your team gathering helps engage others and get buy-in. You can think of the theme as the 'cherry on top of the cake'!

In the real-life example I gave earlier, the theme we gave for this day was: *'Clarity in the midst of Uncertainty'*.

Planning

(Design it right)

By failing to prepare, you are preparing to fail.

- Benjamin Franklin.

Planning a purposeful team gathering is not just about *what* you design for your time together, it's about designing it *right*. And it's not just about what you collaborate on; it's about what participants learn and take away.

I want to emphasise the importance of creating an inclusive, engaging, and purposeful environment when planning and designing workshops. Try and visualise these things and think about participant-centered approaches, fostering connections, and empowering individuals to apply their learning.

WHY PLANNING MATTERS

Facilitating a purposeful team gathering requires intentional planning and design. But there are shortcuts you can take to ensure you design your gathering in the most time-efficient way possible.

Once you have decided on your purpose for your team gathering, the planning part requires sorting through all the ingredients you need, working out which order they need to go in, and what quantities you need – so you deliver the outcomes you desire. At the same time, you're ideally seeing the overall picture as a creative space – so you can flexibly adapt on the day. You'll find that some decisions you make upfront, for example, whether to go virtual or in-person, will be in part determined by the purpose of your gathering.

If you don't plan ahead of time, you're less likely to use your time effectively. You may leave out important details, not factor in specific activities, nor create the necessary space and time for the things you really want to achieve. The gathering is likely to be less engaging and purposeful as a result.

Planning also helps you factor in unforeseen eventualities – they are bound to happen! As the famous saying goes: *Plans are nothing; planning is everything.* Having done some good planning, you will be far more prepared for any eventuality that crops up.

You don't need to plan alone – the best sort of planning happens when you craft ideas in collaboration with others. Involving others, especially the team you're planning for, helps you with the design and helps them to engage in the purpose. If the team doesn't have the time or capacity to help with planning (maybe you've been tasked to do it for them), then try and involve them in a light-touch way and test concepts with them during the planning process.

WHAT'S THE BARE MINIMUM I CAN DO?

Some people avoid planning as they are more comfortable winging it on the day and don't see the benefits of spending too much time or effort in a planning phase. On the other hand, some people can spend too long on planning a gathering instead of just getting on with doing *something*. I reckon there's a sweet spot – planning doesn't necessarily have to take up lots of time, but you want to consider the necessities when designing any gathering, even if these are just the bare essential ingredients.

You might be thinking, 'But I've been to totally unplanned team events and they're great!' Even the most unstructured or seemingly unplanned events require lots of planning! An example of this is hosting *unconferences*. Unconferences are participant-driven gatherings, where the agenda is created by the participants at the beginning of the gathering – anyone who wants to initiate discussion on a topic can claim a time and space. Sure, you don't have to plan an agenda upfront, but there are a whole lot of other factors that you'll want to consider when planning for such an event.

As a bare minimum, consider the essential elements of the 3Ps and their intersections. Keep these in mind with whatever bare minimum planning you plan (!) to do.

Purpose + Planning:

If participants know *why* they're coming to this gathering and have a rough idea of how the time together is going to be spent, they'll know what's expected of them, how to show up, and it'll create **intention** for your gathering.

Planning + Presence:

To ensure participants are engaged and willing to be involved and make stuff happen (**traction**), think about what you'll need to prep them with before, during and after your gathering. Traction literally means creating friction between a body (participants) and its surface (purpose), so think about the bare minimum you need to plan to help participants warm up.

- **Before**: give them a heads up if there's anything they need to think about, or do, before you gather. Is there any pre-work (e.g., an article to read, a question to ponder) that will help them hit the ground running?
- **During**: Starting well is everything – it sets the tone and vibe for the rest of the gathering. You want to design the warm-up well to ensure you create an atmosphere of trust and safety. If you spend some quality time warming up together, you'll be able to tune in to and discern participants' needs and styles throughout the rest of the time you have together. Notice what helps participants to be open? What helps them relax? What are they concerned about, or laughing about?
- **After**: make sure you have a plan for how you'll capture anything that needs follow up after the gathering.

Presence + Purpose:

When participants know why they're there and how they want to show up, they'll be *motivated* to take part. When you plan, think about how you might inject some fun to positively motivate people around the goals you want to achieve. What is going to make people look forward to showing up and feel energised about being there? It could be as simple as crafting a theme for the gathering together; or crowd-sourcing some home-baking to bring along to share.

ESSENTIAL INGREDIENTS FOR PLANNING

It's useful to split the planning stages into three: what you need to do before, during and after. The checklists below help you consider the bare minimum requirements.

Before	☑ Purpose and outcomes
	☑ Frequency of gathering
	☑ Type of gathering (in-person, virtual or hybrid?)
	☑ Calendar invites to all team (plus invited guests)
	☑ Physical logistics – venue, catering, and technology
	☑ Agenda, Runsheet and list of resources required
During	☑ Chunk your time into sections – start well, continue well, finish well
	☑ Time management
	☑ Unexpected elements (e.g. surprises to incorporate)
	☑ Capture moments
	☑ Accountability pauses to capture insights and actions
After	☑ Follow up
	☑ Ask for feedback
	☑ Measure outcomes

QUESTIONS TO CONSIDER

What's the purpose of your gathering?

Is it sharing information, making decisions, discussing complex problems, team building, training, or upskilling, building relationships with others, a strategic planning session, or something else?

What outcomes do you want to achieve?

How do you want the team to think, feel, and behave as a result of the gathering?

Is this a one-off gathering, or something you want to repeat?

Think about the obvious (or not obvious) rituals that help make this team function at its best (e.g., it might be something simple like grabbing a coffee together on Tuesday mornings; or celebrating with cake when a new team member joins) – how might you amalgamate these rituals into your team rhythms? What rhythms would work best? Daily? Weekly? Quarterly? Annually?

Depending on the purpose of your gathering, you may want to commit to a rhythm within your team. Some teams may gather weekly in-person for a 'share, support, and challenge' session; others may do this fortnightly. And sometimes they'll mix it up and invite a guest speaker once a month. Some teams benefit from monthly learning or training sessions on various topics; others have virtual 'pop in' sessions that are come-as-you-are to participate in a Q&A with the leaders. Some invest full days out of the office for quarterly strategic planning sessions. Monthly events might include retrospectives on the previous month and looking forward to the next. Annual gatherings may include reflections, celebrations, and planning for the year ahead.

It's useful if the manager of a team can sit down to plan out an annual calendar of team gathering rhythms in advance. Grab a calendar (or large sheets of flipchart) and start scribbling out important milestones, decision points, and events happening across your team throughout the year. Depending on your team make up and the roles and goals you have, you will know best what rhythms work well for you as a team. On the following page is an example of a team's gathering rhythms.

GATHERING PURPOSE	FREQUENCY	DELIVERY MODE	COMMITMENTS
Governance group	Quarterly	In-person	Consider recommendations; make decisions
1:1s manager-staff	Weekly	In-person or virtual	Wellbeing check-in; progress update on work; support required
Team meeting	Weekly	In-person on even weeks; virtual or hybrid on odd weeks	Share workload; highlight any blockages; provide support for each other; share organisation-wide updates
Training and learning sessions	Monthly	Depends	Learning actions to follow through (for individuals + as a team)
Strategic Planning	Quarterly	In-person	Retrospective on past quarter; goal-setting and confirm priorities and capacity for next quarter; agree on proposals to governance group
Celebrations	Fortnightly + ad-hoc	Depends	Comings and goings of staff (morning tea in-person) On achieving milestones (lunch out as a team at least once a quarter) Fortnightly 'shout out' email from manager to team on progress achieved as a team

In-person, virtual, or hybrid?

We know from research that high-performing teams are ones that spend a lot of time together – so think about how frequently you want your team to gather, and which gatherings need to be in-person, virtual, or hybrid. What type of gathering are you planning for?

- **In-person** (aka 3D gatherings): where everyone is in the same room or physical space together.
- **Virtual**: (aka 2D gatherings): where everyone joins online using digital communication tools (and preferably each individual is on a separate screen or laptop so faces can be clearly seen).
- **Hybrid**: (aka 4D gatherings!): where there's a combination of both in-person and virtual participants.

There's a lot to take into consideration – like the team's goals, constraints, and the individual preferences of team members – when mapping out the frequency and types of team gatherings you have as a team, say, over the course of a year.

The table on the following page shows some of the advantages and disadvantages of different gathering types.

Knowing the delivery mode beforehand makes a significant difference to *how* you design the time together. There are different things you'll want to plan for depending on your delivery mode. Clearly communicating to the team the *type* of gathering you're having helps manage the team's expectations ahead of time.

I've come across examples in the past where an intended in-person gathering has included a virtual/digital joining link in the calendar invitation as well as a room booking location. Some people assume that they can choose to meet virtually for this gathering, but the organiser's intention was to get everyone together in-person, face-to-face in the same room. If

	IN-PERSON	VIRTUAL	HYBRID
ADVANTAGES	• Better connection and engagement • Non-verbal cues • Networking opportunities • Reduced technology dependance • Food to share • Physically interactive, movement	• Accessibility • Cost savings • Time efficiency • Flexibility	• Flexibility for participants • Cost savings • Global collaboration • Adaptability to changing circumstances and preferences for participants
DISADVANTAGES	• Venue and catering costs • Geographical limitations • Travel costs and time • Environmental impact • Limited flexibility for those with scheduling constraints	• Technology issues • Reduced engagement • Limited non-verbal cues • Security concerns	• Technical challenges to integrate both in-person and virtual participants • Balancing engagement • Logistical complexity • Potential inequality between in-person and virtual participants • If there's only one facilitator, it's a high cognitive load for them to manage both in-person and virtual participants (recommend having at least two facilitator roles for this)

the type of gathering is not *clearly* shown in the calendar invitation, don't assume people will know that your intentions are for an in-person, fully virtual, and/or hybrid gathering... make sure you tell them upfront and ahead of time.

Nowadays, we've got increasing modes of flexible work, which means we need to be prepared to adapt how we bring a team together. There are a range of preferences and schools of thought about whether a team needs to meet in-person or if virtually will suffice. I know some leaders tend to prefer in-person meetings only, yet they have a flexible workforce who aren't all in the office at the same time. This means they hardly ever get to gather collectively in-person unless there's a strong commitment to make it happen. I know of other teams who only meet virtually and are suffering from a lack of connection. Being in-person would really help with tackling their social challenges.

If you can avoid hybrid gatherings, do so! I realise they're sometimes inevitable, but I have found that the most effective team gatherings are those where participants are either fully in-person or all virtually attending. With hybrid gatherings, there is so much more you need to prepare for, anticipate, and think about beforehand, and there's extra 'juggle management' required to effectively manage and involve all participants in an inclusive way, so you need to assign more roles to people to ensure you can best facilitate the gathering. It *is* possible to do hybrid gatherings well, but you'll need to make sure you (and those helping you) are confident in using additional tools to manage participant interactions and engagement.

What's the size of your gathering?

Given the numbers of participants attending, what delivery mode would be most practical for this size of gathering?

What venues are available for this gathering size?

What venue will you need?

For in-person gatherings, space and environment are important to helping you achieve the right vibe for your gathering. Think about whether you're seeking a relaxed or formal environment (depending on the purpose and outcomes you're wanting to achieve) and give yourself enough time to book your venue well in advance. Much of the time, venue availability can dictate *when* you can have your gathering, so it's best to organise venue bookings as a first step. A well-chosen venue can make all the difference for creating a positive atmosphere, support collaboration and interaction, and enhance the overall experience for participants. If your budget allows, book somewhere away from your usual workplace – there's nothing better than getting out of the office to help people connect and focus.

The atmosphere of your venue sets the tone for your gathering – think about how you may want to use the space you've got and think creatively about the discussions and activities you want to do together, so you can set up the venue accordingly. Too small a space can feel cramped, whereas too large a space can lead to disengagement. Use the space you've got, and if it's large, perhaps set up 'zones' for the various parts of your gathering (e.g., circle of chairs, breakout spaces, floor-walk spaces, walls with flipcharts). Consider how you place chairs in the room so that people don't have their backs to each other to achieve a more inclusive set up. Depending on the type of gathering you're having, it's good to think about the type of venue you use to host it. For example, a more formal executive gathering may benefit from having table seating where everyone can see each other, have space for laptops etc., whereas a more informal or creative session would benefit with a more relaxed vibe, a flowing breakout space to encourage participants to move around and get into the purpose of the day via more creative and innovative thinking.

For virtual gatherings, think about where you want your team to physically be – will you encourage them to re-position their laptop set up to an alternative space to help reduce distractions and enable you to focus more on your time together? Do you want to encourage 'standing meetings' for virtual gatherings, if people are able to do so? There's science behind this – when we stand, we emit far more positive energy to virtual colleagues than when we sit down slumped at a desk, and it enables us to be more engaged and focused (plus it's a lot better for our health).

If there's going to be a lot of interaction, you'll want participants to have a keyboard set up, perhaps double screens. This all helps with participants feeling like they can see one another easily and interact, and increases engagement overall.

How will you nourish your participants?

Food enhances your time together. Think about how you will nourish the brains in the room. What catering options are available, and what are the team's dietary requirements? It's useful to find out what food options different venues provide, as they deliver at specific times, and this information will help you plan your time together.

Some of the best team gatherings I've been to are those where home-baking is involved – it's a great way of getting your team involved in making the gathering a more informal and inclusive one.

Have you sent a calendar invite out?

An obvious planning task (but it's amazing how many people forget this essential one) is ensuring a calendar invite is sent out to all participants you want to attend. Don't forget to include any external guests in this also (e.g. the external facilitator or guest speaker, if you're having one). In this invitation, communicate the purpose, outcomes, goals and gathering theme to participants. As a bare minimum, communicate the purpose if you haven't worked out the rest yet. Make sure to include who's been invited, and location (i.e. physical venue if in-person, or link if virtual).

Who will you invite and how will you involve them?

There will be some gatherings where you will invite all team members and others where a sub-group of team members will be optimal, depending on its purpose and who you need to be involved.

Involving team members (and externals) in identifying your purpose helps you get more engagement and traction in the end outcomes, not to mention useful feedback along the way to tweak your design before you gather. Get the team involved beforehand, ask for their input on the agenda, purpose, and architecture for the day. It will help them feel more engaged and involved in the outcomes you achieve as a group.

Individual and/or team prework is also useful to do before a gathering, especially if you're going to be tight on time at the actual gathering itself. Choose prework that is realistic given individual contexts and any other constraints. It can be something as simple as a question for everyone to reflect on before you gather to engage their minds beforehand, or it might be an exercise or activity they need to do (as individuals, pairs, or as a team) beforehand that they spend time reflecting on once you gather.

You may also want to invite people from outside of your team to certain gatherings. Thinking about the purpose and outcomes you want to achieve, who are all the other players that align to these things? Maybe they are your stakeholders, key partners, colleagues, guest speakers, or clients – those who will have a lot to contribute to helping your team towards the intended purpose and desired outcomes you want to achieve. It might be a great idea to bring in your boss, or your boss's boss for part of the day – thinking about how you might use them to emphasise the purpose of your gathering.

Make sure you invite external players well in advance, share the purpose and outcomes you're intending for the gathering, what part (if not all) that they're invited to, and what their role will be in attending.

What are the individual preferences and needs of your team members?

Some people prefer face-to-face interactions for building relationships, team cohesion, and being able to read body language in the room. Other people prefer the flexibility, convenience, and efficiency of virtual gatherings. Knowing what the individual preferences are for your team members and how they like to gather, will help you work out what's best for you as a group. It's a great idea to discuss these together as a team.

A note of caution about 'forced fun' – think about how you design your gathering to make it light and fun, but not 'forced fun'. You might recollect 'cringe-worthy' memories of team building activities you've had to endure in the past. How do you get the balance right, yet also get people to step out of their comfort zones and be a little brave? It totally depends on your audience, and we'll go into this in more depth in the next section on Presence.

How can you get everyone's undivided attention?

People are more likely to get distracted during virtual gatherings (multi-tasking on other things) compared to an in-person gathering where 'all tools are down' and there are fewer distractions. If you're meeting virtually, what things can you put in place to help hold the attention of everyone 'in the room' – like ensuring interactions at frequent intervals?

Do you need to discuss any sensitive or controversial topics?

In-person gatherings can be more effective for complex or sensitive discussions, where body language and non-verbal cues are key to building trust. Virtual meetings can be more vulnerable to security breaches, so you need to make sure you have security measures implemented if you're planning on virtually gathering.

Will participants speak and listen one-by-one, or collectively discuss?

Virtual gatherings are great if you want participants to speak one at a time (that's good practice anyway!), but this comes at the cost of having a more rigid agenda. Virtual is not so great for fluent group discussions or creative injections from a group.

There are useful virtual tools you can use for collective conversations so multiple 'voices' can be heard at the same time. Note that any tool you choose will be subject to people's preferences and capabilities to comfortably use it well if it's something they're not already familiar with (sometimes it just needs a bit of practice and patience when you first start).

How long is your gathering?

Gatherings might be anything from 30 minutes long to a full week. How much time do you need? Your purpose and intended outcomes should help you figure that out. Is it a shorter, regular team catch up or is it a more thorough strategic planning session that perhaps requires more time for discussion, reflection, interaction, and participation? Knowing what amount of time you have available, what other constraints there may be on this time, and what you can realistically achieve in the time given, will help you design something fit-for-purpose.

Work out how much time you need to achieve your outcomes. And be realistic!

As a facilitator, I'm often asked to run workshops for teams in pursuit of an array of ambitious outcomes, but they only want to set aside a couple of hours in their day to achieve this work. Rome wasn't built in a day, Boeuf Bourguignon doesn't cook in an hour, and Dream Team Harmony doesn't just magically happen in a 2-hour team building session. It's very common for people to underestimate the time needed for a particular purpose, so think about building space into your agenda to allow for human connection, discussions, and any over-runs. It can also be just as common for people to overestimate the time they need for a particular purpose (e.g. "Why is this a 3-hour meeting when a 20 minute one will cover what's needed on this agenda?").

Longer gatherings (e.g., anything over two hours) are usually best done in-person. If they must be virtual, think about how to manage screen fatigue' risks, and make sure you design in mini breaks. Depending on the length of your gathering, a useful way to plan is to divide your total time up into 'chunks'. You might consider dividing a full day gathering into three or four 1.5-hour sessions with screen breaks (and specific solo-activities for people to carry out during these times and come back and share with the wider group on). A three-day gathering could be divided into six morning/afternoon chunks, each deliberately focusing on a different angle around the purpose and outcomes for this gathering.

When you're planning your gathering, consider the beginning, middle, and end. You want to make sure you start well and finish strong. Our brains have what's called a 'primary and recency' effect, meaning we are more likely to remember either the first or last thing that happened to us in one particular event or setting. Knowing this can help you shake things up a bit in how you plan your gathering time (e.g. if it's a whole day, perhaps split the group up into different zones that switch around halfway through – they'll remember twice as much!).

How are you going to warm up?

Starting your gathering well is one of the most important parts of planning (which is why it's mentioned in the bare essentials above! Think about what will work well as a warm-up for this group considering the type of people you'll have. It's worthwhile getting creative here but be cautious as to whether you warm up with extrovert-friendly icebreakers or something more subtle, depending on the needs of your group. You'll know your people best (but I do encourage you to try something bold).

The timing for warm-ups can be as short as 10 minutes or over an hour depending on what the group needs. I've noticed many team leaders want to make this part as short as possible or skip it entirely so they can get on to the 'real' content of the day – but this is a false assumption. Trust the process you've followed, remembering the outcomes you want to achieve – what will help the team get to these? The better the warm-up goes, the better the synergy of the group, their engagement, trust, and productivity for the remainder of your gathering.

How will you capture moments throughout the gathering?

This may take the form of photos, videos, visual facilitation, screenshots, or notes on flipcharts and whiteboards. It's especially important to capture any specific actions or commitments that the group wants to follow up with (it's amazing how much can get forgotten after a gathering is over!). These will become a tangible output, a useful 'share back' input, and a reminder of the actions and insights after the gathering.

What accessibility considerations do you need to plan for?

Is the team dispersed geographically or across time-zones? If you're planning on meeting in-person, what costs and effort are involved to get everyone to the same place at the same time?

Have you considered the environmental cost of meeting in-person versus virtually? Do the benefits (social connection, body language, being together face-to-face) outweigh the costs associated with gathering in-person?

Are there people with disabilities you need to consider to ensure it's inclusive for everyone taking part?

What technology do you need?

You'll want to know what technology and tools you have at your disposal during the gathering to help you design your time together well. I cannot emphasise how important this is for hybrid gatherings! Find out what the venue offers and how the technology (like screens and sound) is set up and what gadgets you'll need to bring along with you.

I've made mistakes in the past where I've assumed that a room is set up with projectors and equipment, only to turn up just before the start time, to find out that the connection plug for a laptop wasn't there and the batteries for the clicker were dead. It's led to a last minute dash to the electronics store to procure the right gadgets – and arriving to the gathering in a bit of a sweat.

Either avoid the use of technology altogether (wonderful, if you can), or come prepared with a backup plan. It's always helpful to check out a venue a few days before your gathering date, especially if you haven't been there before.

Always give yourself enough time to set up before the start time – it can take longer than you think, especially if you're working in venues with less-than-ideal set ups, or no tech-support person on hand.

If you're reliant on technology, make sure you've got the necessary tools and capability at your disposal for set up and its use. Considering your purpose and intended outcomes, as well as your own tech capability as a facilitator, think about how you want to use technology to enhance your gathering experience. Things like virtual collaboration tools; on-the-fly data analysis and visualisation; access to resources like videos or documents; and even AI recording and documentation are available these days. There are so many options now available over and above the old-fashioned 'death by PowerPoint' type of gathering.

Virtual gatherings benefit from a solid internet connection, one person per laptop/screen (cameras on), and some form of participant interactive tool (over and above just the chat function). There are some great interactive tools out there to encourage participation (like Slido, Mentimeter and Miro,[9] to name just a few). As a facilitator of a virtual gathering, it benefits participants if you've got an excellent sound set up and lighting to help run the gathering well. Be clear, visible and easy-to-understand.

Hybrid gatherings require a lot more planning and preparation around technology – like a good screen and sound set up in the room (for in-person participants to be able to hear and see virtual participants, and vice versa). Interactive collaboration and participation tools for both in-person and virtual participants are a must – so everyone can engage on a level playing field.

What unexpected elements can you incorporate into the gathering?

Injecting some moments of surprise into your time together leads to anticipatory energy. Examples could be things like a team building activity over lunchtime, a treasure hunt, a delicious food surprise, some form of competition, sharing photos, or interspersing spontaneous energisers throughout the day.

How will you finish well?

Make sure you finish strong, with time built in to 'end'. It's useful to end gatherings with some actions and accountability, to recap on any captured moments. This could be a quick-fire 'Like, Wish, Wonder' exercise – grab a flipchart and pen (or virtual whiteboard if you're all online), and ask the team to spend some time at the end sharing back things they *liked* about the gathering, things they *wished* for (that didn't happen), and things that they're still left *wondering* about. This is also a great exercise to help shape ideas for your next gathering.

How will you follow up?

Always make sure you follow up with the team afterwards. You want to create stickability and accountability from your team gathering. Following up is the icing on the cake; it adds that extra layer of sweetness and ensures the experience is complete.

Make sure to follow up with a short recap (of actions and commitments)within 48 hours of the gathering, while everything is still fresh in people's minds. This can be as simple as sharing a photo of the whiteboard you wrote these on – they don't always need to be typed up! It's a helpful reminder to participants of each other's insights and any actions that came from the gathering. Sharing commitments and actions helps create momentum, meaning, and traction while everything is still fresh in the team's hearts and minds.

Ask for feedback – and respond to it. You may like to have a set of your own questions that you always ask after each gathering, or ask specific questions about the outcomes and goals you set for a particular gathering (how successful were you in achieving these as a team on a scale of 1-10?).

There's a set of feedback questions I often use in the resources library on my website (antoniamilkop.com/resources).

RESOURCES YOU'LL NEED

Having a good list of resources that you'll need on the day is essential to making sure you're well prepared ahead of time. When designing your gathering, take notes of any specific resources that you'll need for the different activities during your gathering (even if it's something small like blu tack, you'll thank yourself for noting these things down and organising them beforehand).

Agendas and Runsheets – some useful templates

All gatherings need an agenda. And many, but not all gatherings, benefit from a runsheet. There's sometimes confusion about the difference between an agenda and a runsheet, and different terminology that's used. Here's my clarification:

- **Agenda**: outlines a high-level view of topics or items to be discussed during a gathering – it serves as a guide for what will be covered and in what order. It is your 'big-picture' view of the gathering.
- **Runsheet:** is a more detailed document that provides a more time-specific schedule and details – its purpose is to help the facilitator(s) ensure that every aspect of the gathering runs smoothly.

You'll find examples of an Agenda and Runsheet in the resources library on my website (antoniamilkop.com/resources).

I always design the agenda first – and discuss this with others (or get approval if needed), before going into designing the more detailed runsheet. A draft agenda is a good tool for confirming purpose and getting to the essence of what's wanted. Once you've got your agenda finalised, the runsheet should be a lot easier. It's a great idea to socialise your agenda with team members for their contributions beforehand, asking them to vote or choose options. All these things help create buy-in and enable the team to get more involved in the purpose and outcomes for your gathering.

It's helpful to look at the total time you've got allocated for your gathering, and to break this down into chunks of time. Reflecting on what you're wanting to achieve, divide your time into the chunks you think you'll need to achieve these things, and assign how long each section, activity, or discussion will likely take (make sure you build in some space to your time scheduling also).

A good agenda should include:

- The title of your gathering and theme
- Name of the team
- Date, time, location/venue
- Attendees' names (include any known absences) and any external attendees you're inviting
- Facilitator
- Purpose and goals
- Pre-work
- What to bring with you
- A high-level run through of timing for how the gathering is 'chunked'

Once you've agreed on the flow and timing of your agenda, you can start outlining the more specific details for your runsheet.

A good runsheet will include the same as the above agenda as well as:

- Useful facilitator notes (and specific details or role clarity if there is more than one facilitator – i.e. who is leading or supporting various sessions).
- Extra details and timeframes for the start time and finish time (for set up and pack up) and ensuring the venue is booked for this time. When outlining your activities, make sure you build in extra time – for example, for nature breaks, activities that may run under or over time. As a rule of thumb, I build in five minutes of extra time per 30-minute activity.
- When designing the activities for your 'chunks', think about the

overall architecture of the space you'll have at the venue, and get creative with ideas for how you might use the main space and any breakout spaces you'll have effectively throughout the day. For example, will any furniture need to be moved around during the day, and when is the best time to do this?

- A detailed list of resources you'll need for each of the activities throughout your gathering.
- A list of any other additional items, useful notes, or web links that you need access to on the day.

Presence

(Harness the energy)

He aha te mea nui o te ao? He tangata, he tangata, he tangata!
(What is the most important thing in the world? It is the people!)

- Māori proverb

You know your purpose, you've planned some logistics, now you need to think about the intangible factors that affect your gathering and the most important part – the people!

The success of your gathering will rely heavily on harnessing the energy of everyone that is taking part. You want to harness the group's energy in a way that ensures people feel engaged, want to participate, are included, feel safe, and are genuinely connected to the gathering's purpose.

It's a bit of an art to harness energy well in a group of people (and even more so in a virtual or hybrid setup!) – it's why master facilitators get paid well to do their jobs. It takes skill, experience, empathy, impartiality, and objectivity – as well as being receptive and responsive to the verbal and non-verbal feedback that's happening throughout the gathering.

I've been writing most of this book while living in France, where the art of bread making is passed down through generations for good reason. In addition to the knowledge and skills required for good bread making, there's also plenty of intuition involved, allowing artisans to adjust on the fly, such as modifying hydration levels or fermentation times based on how the dough feels and behaves. There's a level of mastery and dedication to the craft, and it's a hugely competitive industry in France.

So, if we think of 'presence' as being a bit like the art of bread making – being able to use intuition to make adjustments on the fly, according to how a team is feeling or behaving – what are the essential tools that will help you do this?

I've boiled this chapter down into the tools I've found most useful in harnessing presence in a team. There are easy things to become aware of to help you harness people's energy so that you can adapt your own facilitation style to best harness energy at a gathering and bring out the best in a team.

- **Dynamics**: Know the people dynamics within the team.
  - What types of people energy will you have at your gathering (high – low; positive - negative)?
  - Are there any tensions in the team dynamics you'll need to take into account?

- **Self-awareness**: Know yourself
  - What are your strengths and style as a facilitator?
  - How can you use your strengths and energy, trusting your instincts about what's going on, and create agency and authority in facilitating the way the team participates?

- **Roles**: Know the roles everyone will play at the gathering.
  - I don't mean people's 'job positions' but more specifically who is in the room and what are the roles various people are going to be playing at the gathering? – e.g., facilitator, energizer-bunny,

timekeeper, venue oversight, challenger, bridge builder, tech buddy, deep thinker). Have you thought about what hat everyone might wear and how everyone will play together?

WHY PRESENCE MATTERS

Energy flows where attention goes.

- Tony Robbins

I've experienced plenty of gatherings as an attendee, which were lacking in presence. There was a clear purpose for the gathering, everyone knew why they were there, and what outcomes they wanted to get out of it. There was a clear agenda and a thoughtful plan for the day, with specific goals to be accomplished. Participants came along knowing what to expect but the energy on the day was totally lacking. The style and vibe of the gathering didn't resonate well with the participants in the room; it wasn't engaging and didn't really engender generate participant feedback. And, worst of all, there were plenty of cringeworthy moments across the day. The differing needs of the group hadn't been catered for.

During these times it felt incredibly frustrating and time-wasting for me and others to be there. It would have been great if the facilitator could have interacted with the people-energy: tuned into *who* they were delivering to and *how* to best create traction with a group like this to motivate and engage them.

I've also found another common 'energy-sucking' culprit of gatherings is a lack of identified roles at the outset. You may turn up to a purposeful gathering that's been well designed and put together 'by committee', but no one has remembered to take responsibility for making the gathering itself run well (room set up, tech, identifying a chair etc.). To make a gathering successful and engaging, it's important to identify any essential roles that are needed to make things run smoothly (see Roles we Play later in this section).

It's not just the person who is facilitating the gathering – they're not solely responsible for presence. Everyone is. Every individual present at a gathering brings different energy to the group; and a safe space will allow participants to share, engage, and work together collaboratively.

Before you gather, it's useful to discuss with participants and encourage them to think about the roles they play at a gathering. I find this especially important for those in leadership positions – people will look to you and follow so how are you thinking about showing up and role-modelling at the gathering itself?

TYPES OF PEOPLE ENERGY

**How do you manage the people energy in the room
to ensure you can get the best out of everyone?**

When facilitating a team gathering, you'll probably be dealing with a multitude of different energy types in the room. You'll want to be aware of these, and cater for the activities, types, and levels of participation you expect from others accordingly.

There's a common misperception that high energy = good energy. This is not always the case. There's the obvious, and heavily researched, introvert-extrovert dynamic. In team gathering settings, introverts may struggle to have their voices heard or find opportunities to contribute their perspectives, or they may find social interactions draining and have a preference for more intimate one-on-one connections with their colleagues.

If introverts are not actively participating in discussions, they may be misunderstood as aloof or indifferent. On the other hand, extroverts may be perceived as dominating discussions, making impulsive decisions, or overcommitting to work goals on behalf of the whole team.

People are diverse, and different people have different energy levels based on natural variations in their personality and temperaments. What matters most is self- and group-awareness of this and finding ways to align and adapt our own facilitator energy to different circumstances.

Different types of energy

The quadrant below outlines some of the common energy dynamics that I've come across in team settings – between high-energy and low-energy people and the results of that tension – both positive and negative.

As the facilitator, the more aware you can be of energy dynamics at play, the more you will be able to harness the presence of people by adapting your own style and approach.

What you might observe as 'negative energy' might be a precursor to the twin of 'positive energy' – it may just need harnessing to bring it into the positive sense (think of solar versus wind power).

I believe it's the facilitator's role to help guide and shift the energy during a gathering and to help create safe spaces for people to connect. It is not the facilitator's role to change people's mindsets but there are things you can do to help others reframe how they might be thinking, feeling, or behaving based on what you may observe during a gathering.

	Negative	Positive
High Energy	The Restless Challenger	The Open-hearted Enthusiast
Low Energy	The Realistic Cynic	The Reflective Thinker

	Negative	Positive
High Energy	Impulsive Restless Difficulty focussing Impatient Overcommitment Inattentive to detail Overwhelms others	Active and energetic Enthusiastic Motivated Social and outgoing Optimistic Initiative taker Adventurous Productive
Low Energy	Reserved or withdrawn Lacking initiative Tends to procrastinate Resistent to change Struggles with fast pace Potentially unmotivated Perceived as anti-social	Calm Reflective Patient Deep thinker Focussed Empathetic Supportive

All teams are different and develop their own unique DNA. Find out beforehand what the strengths of the team are, what energises and motivates them, and what needs they have. Make sure you discuss this with the leader and/or some team members before you gather with them, so you can tailor the activities accordingly to what you think are the best fit.

For example, some teams will have more 'high energy' members among them and enjoy lots of team building activities and interactivity at a faster pace, with music on in the background. Other teams will have more low-energy team members and may appreciate more contemplative and reflective exercises, breakout spaces and opportunities to reflect in pairs before providing their input together in a group setting.

> *Every individual is a unique masterpiece, a mosaic of experiences, qualities, and potential waiting to be discovered.*

You won't be able to cater perfectly to everyone's needs in the room for every minute of your time together. But you will be able to design a mix of activities that cater to the various needs and preferences of the group, depending on the mix of styles, preferences, and temperaments.

TEAMS AS SYSTEMS

How can you treat a team as a whole, and, at the same time, cater to the needs of a group of individuals? When you're facilitating a team gathering, you want to consider both. Team members are inter-related, so it's important to consider the team as a whole rather than a collection of parts. I refer to this concept as the 'team DNA'.

It's like the difference between the individual ingredients in a recipe when they're set out and ready to be put together, compared to the end result when you combine all these ingredients together and to cook. Flour, sugar, butter, eggs, and milk. Separately they're one thing, mixed together methodically and cooked to perfection, they can be a whole lot more.

There's a wide variety of diagnostic assessments and tools publicly available – some are available for free, but most of the good ones have a cost associated with them as the organisations that produce them invest in creating robust methodology and algorithms, alongside cutting-edge research. These assessments help teams discover more about 'what makes them tick' and build awareness of people as individuals and collectively as a team.

CLIFTONSTRENGTHS® - WHAT'S THE TEAM'S DNA?

What will happen when we think about what is right with people rather than fixating on what is wrong with them?

- Donald Clifton

One of my favourite tools to use in coaching individuals and teams is the CliftonStrengths®10 tool (formally known as StrengthsFinder). It's an online psychometric assessment tool, developed by Gallup, which measures an individual's natural talents – their natural patterns of thinking, feeling, and behaving. This tool is used for personal and professional development by individuals and organisations across the world (at the time of writing this book, over 31 million people across the globe have completed a CliftonStrengths® assessment).

Donald Clifton (a pioneer in the field of positive psychology and strengths-based psychology) started developing the tool in the 1950s but the tool itself wasn't publicly released until 2001. There's a lot of meta-studies and science behind CliftonStrengths®, which explains why it's so widely recognised across the globe as a useful tool to better understand and ignite potential in individuals and teams.

CliftonStrengths® aligns with principles of positive psychology, emphasising the importance of focusing on what individuals do well and finding ways to apply their strengths in various aspects of work and life. The tool also helps in highlighting blind spots in individuals and teams, and providing a tool to best manage these.

Since its introduction, CliftonStrengths® has become a widely used tool for personal development, leadership development, team building, and organisational improvement. There are thousands of qualified Gallup-certified Strengths Coaches across the world (including me), who coach individuals, teams, and organisations in discovering and developing their strengths.

This tool is not only very useful for individuals in helping them become more aware of their own strengths and how to apply them; it's also an incredibly useful tool for teams to discover how they work best together as a whole.

When you aggregate the strengths assessment profiles of everyone in a team into a combined summary, you can easily identify what their dominant strengths are and understand what motivates and energises the group as a whole. You can also identify what is likely to get in the way of a team's performance.

A team summary of strengths can also identify the 'unique contributors' in the team's DNA (think of these people being a bit like the magic ingredient) where perhaps only one individual possesses a particular dominant strength in their profile – they have a valuable role to play in bringing the benefits of that that strength to the team as a whole. When the team is considered as a system, you can start spotting powerful partnerships (combinations of strengths between individuals) that exist in the team – and you're now really thinking about the team as a system in order to bring out their best.

When organising team gatherings, I've found the CliftonStrengths® tool not only useful for growing a team's self-awareness and appreciation of each other, but, as a facilitator, it also helps you tune into the team DNA in the way you might choose to approach how you facilitate the team according to the strengths make-up of the team.

Most of the teams I've worked with have benefited a great deal from learning their CliftonStrengths®, well beyond the gathering event itself. They continue to use a shared, common language around strengths in their everyday interactions with one another in a very constructive, positively framed way. It's one of the best tools I've used when facilitating team gatherings in helping teams discover how they can best work together, share resources, and understand each other's natural talents to direct them towards what they do best.

TUCKMAN'S MODEL – WHAT PHASE IS THE TEAM IN?

Teamwork makes the dream work.

- John Maxwell

Bruce Tuckman's phases of team development framework[11] is another useful tool to help identify the phase a team is currently at in its development. It's a well-recognised framework, first introduced by Bruce Tuckman in 1965. It has since been expanded on by various researchers, including Scott M. Graffius (2021), who introduced characteristics and proven strategies for each of the phases.[12] The framework can be used in the context of team building, group dynamics, and organisational development to help teams and leaders understand and navigate the challenges and dynamics that occur as groups form and work together toward common goals.

The framework describes the stages that teams go through as they 'form, storm, norm, and perform'. This understanding helps to figure out ways to best facilitate a gathering, depending on the phase a team is currently in.

- **Forming**: In the forming stage, group members come together, often with a sense of excitement and anticipation. However, they may not yet be familiar with each other, and there may be a degree of anxiety and uncertainty. During this stage, members tend to be polite and cautious in their interactions, and they may look to the group leader for guidance and direction.
- **Storming**: The storming stage is characterised by increased conflict and tension among group members. As members get to know each other better, differences in opinions, personalities, and working styles become apparent. This can lead to disagreements, power struggles, and challenges to the group's authority or structure. Effective leadership and conflict resolution skills are essential during this phase.
- **Norming**: In the norming stage, the group begins to establish norms, values, and shared expectations. Members start to resolve their differences and develop a sense of cohesion. They work together more harmoniously and become more accepting of each other's ideas and contributions. This stage is marked by increased cooperation and a sense of unity.
- **Performing**: The performing stage is when the group is at its most productive. Members have resolved their conflicts, established effective communication, and are able to collaborate efficiently. They focus on achieving the group's goals and tasks. Leadership

Tuckman's model - the stages of teams

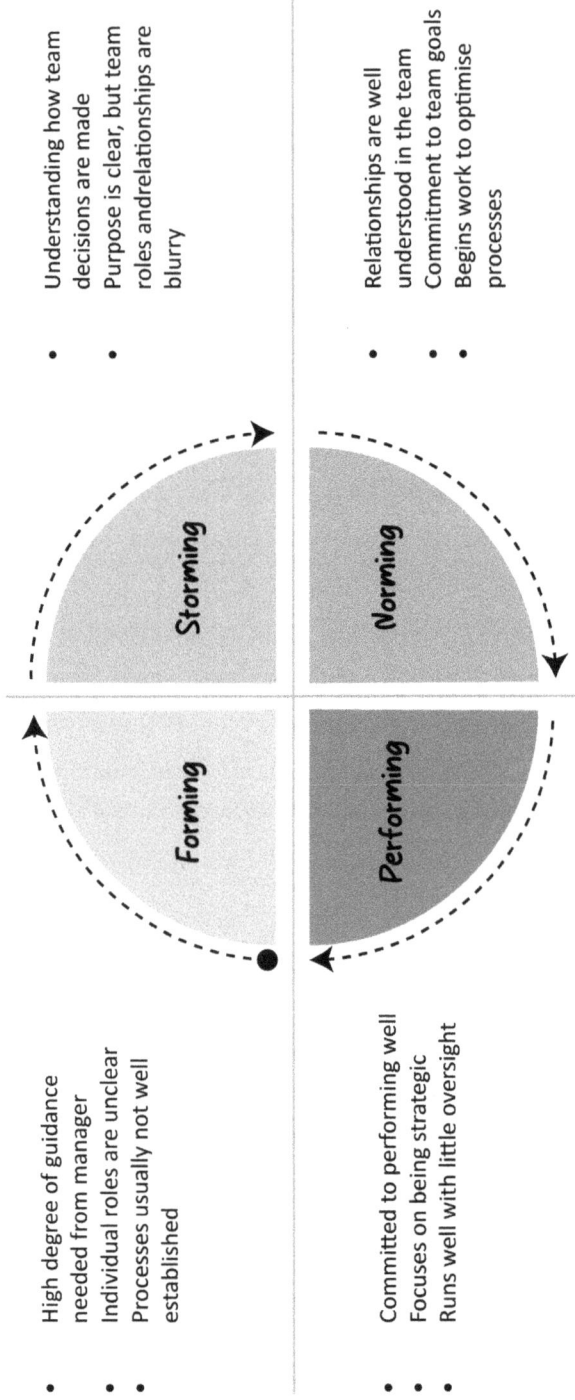

- Understanding how team decisions are made
- Purpose is clear, but team roles and relationships are blurry

- Relationships are well understood in the team
- Commitment to team goals
- Begins work to optimise processes

Storming

Norming

Forming

Performing

- High degree of guidance needed from manager
- Individual roles are unclear
- Processes usually not well established

- Committed to performing well
- Focuses on being strategic
- Runs well with little oversight

Model inspired by and adapted from Bruce Tuckman's and Scott M. Graffius Phases of Team Development work.

may become more shared among members, and the group operates as a cohesive unit.

- **Adjourning** (or Mourning): In some variations of the model, an adjourning stage is included. This stage represents the disbanding or dissolution of the group after its goals have been achieved or its purpose fulfilled. During this stage, members may experience a sense of closure and reflect on their accomplishments. It can be accompanied by feelings of sadness or loss, especially if the group has become close-knit.

Teams don't necessarily go through the phases linearly or experience each phase in the same way. Some teams may skip or revisit stages, and the duration of each phase can vary significantly. Additionally, external factors, such as changes to the team, restructures, or onboarding new team members, can influence the team's development.

When you're planning a team gathering, observe where you think the team is currently at in the phases of its development. Discern what type of support, guidance, or assistance they may need in the way you design and facilitate the gathering. The following diagram illustrates what types of behaviours, needs, and motivations you might notice in a team during each stage, it helps you understand the potential challenges and opportunities a team might face depending on which stage of the journey they are in.

What types of behaviours, needs, and motivations might you notice in a team during each stage?

As people come together, energy and enthusiasm are high. 'Playing nice' with one another, potential aversion to conflict.

- Information gathering phase
- Striving to understand objectives, roles, responsibilities
- Visibility
- Big picture
- Communicating success criteria

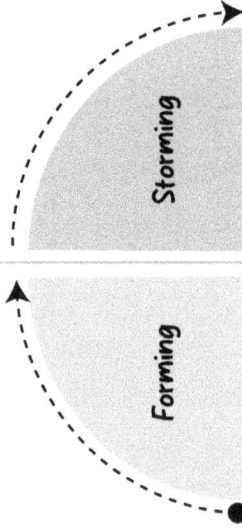

Remember that storming is a normal and necessary part for teams to become effective.

- Requesting and encouraging feedback
- Resolving conflict
- Identifying issues and facilitating their resolution
- Normalising matters
- Building trust by honouring commitments

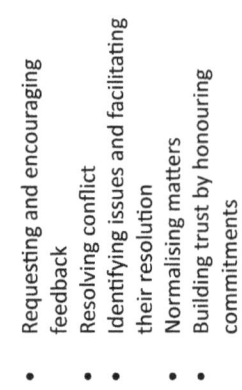

Appreciating each other's strengths and lean into one another, resolving differences to create real results.

- Recognising individual and team efforts
- Providing learning opportunities and feedback
- Monitoring the 'energy' of the team

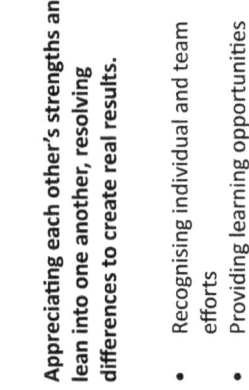

'In the zone', work flows easily.

- Guiding from the side (minimal intervention)
- Celebrating successes
- Encouraging collective decision-making and problem-solving
- Eliminate road bumps and friction

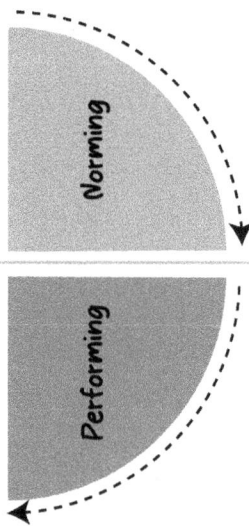

Storming

Norming

Forming

Performing

Model inspired by and adapted from Bruce Tuckman's and Scott M. Graffius Phases of Team Development work.

YOUR PRESENCE + THEIR PRESENCE

> *Your energy is contagious.*
> *Either you affect people or you infect people.*

You can't control anyone else's energy, but you can control your own and how your energy influences others.

As the facilitator of a gathering, you need to be mindful of your own energy and emotions. The demeanour you bring can greatly influence the team atmosphere in the room. You can intentionally direct your own energy and attention to help bring out the best in a team.

Pay attention to the team's dynamics and adapt your facilitation style accordingly. Trust your instincts about when a group may need a different approach (e.g., more relaxed versus a more structured approach; smaller breakout discussions versus bigger group discussions; interactive 'stand up' activities versus quiet reflections and note-taking). You can adapt the activities to help achieve the outcomes the team is seeking, while ensuring you bring out the best in everyone.

Knowing yourself

It's important to understand your own strengths as a facilitator and learn how to aim your strengths in ways that bring value to and benefit others, while at the same time managing your weaknesses or any 'dark sides' your strengths may have!

If you are not fully aware of what your strengths are, there are some great online tools out there that can help you discover your unique strengths and learn more about your own facilitation style. The CliftonStrengths® tool, which I've referred to earlier in this section, is one of the most life-transforming assessments I've done in building my own self-awareness and appreciation of my strengths as a facilitator. Knowing my strengths and weaknesses better, I'm able to be more conscious in the unique ways I bring service to others and manage some of the things that others may find challenging about my style and methods!

> I am someone who loves going at a fast pace, putting thoughts into action straight away (Activator), exploring lots of different options for ways of doing things (Strategic, always have a back up plan!), and pivoting on the spot with ideas and options people are considering (Arranger) to make sure we get the most out of our time together (Maximizer). As well as having an infectious enthusiasm for life (Positivity), I'm also pretty task-focused and like to get things done on time (Achiever), and take ownership in doing so (Responsibility). I also tend to spend lots of time tailoring team gatherings to a specific audience (Individualization) to make sure it's fit-for-purpose for them. I get lots of satisfaction over seeing other people's progression and encouraging growth in others (Developer) – it's probably what contributes to the 'encourage-ment energy' that I share with others.
>
> All these things are great strengths as a facilitator, but if I'm facilitating a group that doesn't share the same strengths as me, my style might overwhelm their experience and come across as hurried, cluttered, or maybe even superficial. They might prefer to be more reflective, have time to digest and consider topics, spend longer on the context and rationale behind decisions, and tackle one issue at a time before moving on to the next thing. They might also want to spend more time in building relational connections with each other and may feel I'm 'rushing' them on to the next task.
>
> This type of self-awareness of 'knowing myself' is useful for me to reflect on beforehand and make sure I can adapt my own style of facilitation to best suit the needs of the group.

Check list tips for managing energy

It's fun to experiment with harnessing people energy in gatherings. It's easier than you might think, with a few key tips and tricks.

1. **Create a safe space – from the start**

You want to create an atmosphere where participants feel safe expressing their ideas and opinions, without fear of criticism or judgment. When people feel heard and respected, the energy tends to be much more positive. The venue set up, welcome, warm up, and other activities you do are important in creating this safe space at the start, breaking the ice, and boosting energy levels.

2. **Be clear and specific with your purpose and objectives**

At the start of your gathering, recap the purpose and objectives for your gathering. This helps everyone understand why they're there and stay focussed on this purpose.

3. **Determine the level of commitment of the team**

What's the level of commitment the team wishes to put into this gathering? At the end of the day, it's their choice – and, as the old adage goes. – the more they put in, the more they'll get out. You can gauge the team's commitment by asking permission-seeking questions upfront. Some simple questions to ask (get the team to give their scores of 1-10 for these questions):
   - What level of energy do you want to put in to today?
   - How much do you expect to get out of today?

4. **Establish 'rules of engagement' at the start of your gathering – together as a team**

A bit like ground rules, these will help manage expectations of the group throughout your gathering, and may include things like active listening, respecting other's opinions, staying on topic. It's worth noting that there may be spoken and unspoken ground rules – try and extract what you can upfront and discern from the group what they might need in order to make the space of your gathering an energising and positive experience.

5. Engage everyone

Ensure that everyone has a chance to participate. You might encourage quieter participants to share their thoughts or ideas, or actively manage more dominant voices to prevent one or a few individuals monopolising a conversation. But be careful how you do this as more introverted types may not appreciate being put on the spot and asked to contribute something in a group setting. Alter how you do your various activities throughout the gathering to create different ways in which people can contribute (e.g., spoken, written, reflective).

6. Positive framing

Use positive framing and language to keep the energy upbeat. You can encourage the participants to focus on solutions rather than dwelling on problems.

7. Energy checks

It's worth periodically gauging the energy levels throughout your gathering. You can ask participants specific questions to check in on this or observe visual cues to assess the group's energy and adjust your approach as needed to re-energise the group if energy levels dip. A 'battery level' indicator is a useful check-in tool and helps identify and manage the group's energy as well as catering to individual needs.

8. Encourage feedback

It's worth seeking regular feedback from participants on your facilitation. What's working for you? What's not? It shows you value their input and want to make the time work well for them.

9. Stay neutral

As a facilitator, your role is to guide the group, not impose your own opinions or biases. Stay neutral and impartial to maintain the team's trust and positive energy. This is more challenging if you are facilitating your own gathering *and* you are a key contributor of the team (i.e., you haven't brought an external facilitator in). If this is the case for you it's important that you define to everyone (out loud) what 'hat' you are wearing at different stages throughout your gathering.

10. Celebrate achievements

Make sure you acknowledge and celebrate the team's progress and achievements throughout the gathering. Genuine, positive reinforcement goes a long way, and can really boost the energy and motivation of participants.

11. Manage conflict gracefully

Conflict is a natural part of team dynamics. When conflicts arise, make sure you address them constructively and encourage open dialogue. I've dedicated a whole chapter to this later in this section (*Managing Conflict*).

12. Trust your gut

Lastly, trust your own instincts about what will work or won't work with a particular team, based on your diagnosis of them and what they need. There may be some activities you think would work well with this team, but there is a 'nervousness' about doing them as it may be out of the comfort zone for some or all of the participants. If you feel confident leading these activities, know that they'll make a positive impact on the outcomes you're seeking, and can trust the process in leading them, then do so! I've had lots of examples in the past where the manager of a team is slightly nervous about doing an activity. When these activities are led well – in a safe space – it's been incredible how much benefit the team has gotten from doing them.

THE ROLES WE PLAY

It takes a whole team to run a purposeful team gathering. Figuring out the roles everyone plays on the day, and how everyone can play to their strengths, will help you facilitate purposeful team gatherings.

Depending on the complexity and size of your gathering, I've highlighted below what I think are some of the key roles in organising a purposeful team gathering. Often these roles can be spread out or shared across just a few people, but the most important thing is to make sure all these roles are accounted for when you're planning your gathering if you want it to run smoothly.

Initiator Facilitator(s) Logistical superhero Participants Communications Health and Safety Technology support Leaders and/or managers External guests

Initiator	The person who is responsible for initiating the gathering and making it happen, as well as communicating the purpose and outcomes sought (this is usually the manager or team leader).
Facilitator(s)	Responsible for planning and running the gathering, guiding everyone through the agenda, facilitating discussions and activities, managing energy flow, transitions between different parts of the day, and making sure timing stays on track. Depending on the size of the team, or complexity of the gathering, you may need more than one facilitator
Logistical superhero	Oversees logistics, like venue booking and set up, budget, catering, travel logistics, coordination of resources and any equipment that's needed. They make sure everything is in place at the gathering and runs smoothly.
Communications	Responsible for ensuring the right people are invited and sharing any necessary information and materials before and after.
Technology support	Responsible for supporting set up and any troubleshooting of equipment and software during the gathering. For virtual or hybrid gatherings, I recommend you assign a 'tech-buddy' role that assists participants who are attending virtually.
Health and Safety	Responsible for ensuring that safety measures are in place and communicates emergency procedures to all participants (as well as things like ensuring the heating, cooling, or ventilation is optimal throughout your gathering).
Participants	The team members themselves (the most important role in the gathering!) Responsible for turning up and coming prepared to participate in the purpose of the gathering. In some cases, they may help support the design of the gathering, including its purpose and outcomes, and may help with running some of the activities.
External guests	Participants may also include external guests that are invited for specific reasons or to present or speak on a specific topic.
Leaders and/or managers	Responsible for setting the tone of the gathering, role-modelling, and promoting the purpose and outcomes you want the team to achieve on the day.

MANAGING CONFLICT

When facilitating team gatherings, you're bound to experience lots of different team dynamics and will need to manage any conflict or awkward moments that crop up. I've written quite a bit in this chapter as I think it's especially important and often mis-diagnosed, or avoided altogether.

Teams experience natural conflict for a variety of reasons, and, as a facilitator of any team gathering, it's important for you to be aware of what potential conflict may already exist or is likely to crop up during a gathering (you won't be able to predict all of it, but it's useful to be prepared to manage it when it does crop up).

Conflict is a healthy thing, when managed well. It stimulates creativity and innovation, encourages open communication and debate, strengthens relationships and trust between team members, and identifies problems early so they can be addressed. When conflict is managed poorly, it will erode trust, stifle creativity and collaboration, harm productivity, create stress, and undermine morale in a team. So, as facilitator, you'll want to think about how to manage conflict well in a team.

Common reasons for conflict

I've outlined below some of the common reasons as to why conflict occurs in teams (there's plenty of research and books written on each of these topics, so I'd recommend exploring further if one or more of these is demonstrated in your team):

Interpersonal dynamics
- **Personality clashes:** differences in personality traits, like whether someone is an introvert or extrovert, can lead to clashes in their communication styles and working preference.

- **Conflict of interest:** if team members have conflicting personal or professional interests, this can impact in the way they collaborate or make decisions.
- **Lack of trust:** essential for team cohesion, the absence of trust leads to defensiveness or suspicion.
- **Cultural differences:** varied values, norms, expected behaviours, and communication styles contribute to misunderstandings in a team.
- **Diverse perspectives:** teams are (ideally) composed of individuals with different backgrounds, experiences, and viewpoints. We all approach problems or decisions from different angles.

Role and goal clarity

- **Unclear roles and responsibilities:** when team members are unsure about their roles or what's expected of them, it can lead to misunderstanding and disagreements about who should be doing what.
- **Misaligned goals:** if team members have conflicting goals or priorities, it can create tension and stifle cooperation.
- **Leadership problems:** poor leadership can cause confusion and frustration. 'Leadership issues' are the scapegoat teams often use for the reasons behind their existing conflict – yes, effective leadership is vitally important, but you can see from the whole of this list, it's not the only thing that contributes to conflict in teams.

Resource management and environmental factors

- **Competition for resources:** when there are limited resources (time, money, or even recognition), it can create conflicts as team members compete for their 'fair share'.
- **External pressures:** external factors, like tight deadlines,

high-stake projects, doing work in a national crisis can increase stress levels in a team and make conflicts more likely.

- **Change and uncertainty:** major changes, restructures, or organisational realignment can create uncertainty among a team, leading to increased conflict.
- **Communication issues:** poor communication or miscommunication and a lack of transparency can breed misunderstandings and conflicts within a team.

Historical factors

- **Performance issues:** uneven or mediocre performance by some team members can cause resentment and frustration amongst others.
- **Past conflicts:** unresolved conflicts from the past can resurface and compound current issues.

Why conflict is healthy (when it's managed well)

Managing conflict well means you can, like a skilful chef, blend seemingly disparate ingredients to create a delicious dish. Poorly managed conflict is like a kitchen in disarray, a chaotic environment where chefs work against each other, things are burnt, and kitchen mishaps aren't remedied – a recipe for disaster!

Lots of us want to shy away when we bump up against the awkwardness of conflict in a team, but constructive conflict is great. Managed well, conflict in a team leads to increased trust, collaboration, problem solving, productivity, innovation, creativity, and improved team dynamics. On the flip side, unaddressed or poorly managed conflict can tip the scales and erode all these things.

**Team gatherings are an excellent opportunity
to navigate and resolve conflict well.**

The facilitator has a responsibility to ensure that any existing or new conflicts that arise are well managed during the gathering – especially if these conflicts are causing the outcomes of your gathering to go off-track.

I was facilitating an in-person team gathering of 10 people. During the second hour of our gathering (it was an all-day gathering), I noticed there appeared to be a lot of people-tension in the room – via body language, muttered words, and some sharp comments shared between individuals. It appeared that there was some unresolved conflict between a few of the team members (which also affected the rest of the team).

As the external facilitator, I had no idea what the issue(s) were – I could just sense them (I don't think the manager had been that upfront with me beforehand about what was going on in the team, or maybe they were unaware of it).

When the next sharp comment was made, I brought things to the attention of the group – is there something unresolved going on here? Would you like to discuss it together as a team? Cue: some uncomfortable silence and awkward side-glances. This issue was outside of the purpose of the gathering itself, but it seemed to be affecting the positive energy and desired outcomes we wanted to get out of our time together (improved ways of working together as a team).

It was evident that there was appetite in the room from most (but not all) of the team members to address this issue upfront. So, I put the challenge out to the team – did they want to continue dialogue on this issue (even though it wasn't part of our gathering's agenda)? We could give ourselves the next 30 minutes to talk through things openly and in a safe space, and shave off some time from the other parts of the day. With these time-bounds, there was overall agreement from the group to spend the next half hour addressing and discussing this conflict.

I asked questions and gave space for those who wanted to speak to speak and be heard. After just 10 minutes of discussion, it was evident that some unaddressed issues had been swept under the carpet for quite some time and hadn't been addressed in a constructive manner. The issues were due to poor communication – team members weren't being transparently communicated with. Things they needed to know were coming as a surprise to them, or from side angles via communication from other people in the organisation. For example, when new staff were joining the team, what change updates were going on in the organisation, who was doing what roles (additional role clarity issues). This had led to a lack of trust in their leader and increased defensiveness and suspicion amongst team members.

The team decided that they needed more transparent communications from their leader – he agreed to forward on senior management updates to the rest of the team on a weekly basis, and keep abreast of communicating updates regarding staff changes in the team with team members first before the rest of the group. Some of the team members also requested more opportunities for more frequent manager-staff one-on-one catch ups (these had taken a bit of a backburner in recent times or been cancelled at the last minute, due to other pressing demands and deadlines). It was agreed that 1:1 catch ups with staff needed to be treated as a priority.

The result? Just by having this conversation as a team, the actual issue, or conflict, was identified and the team generated some solutions to resolve it. The level of tension (specifically, suspicion and defensiveness between team members) seemed to reduce and over the lunch break the group had a better overall vibe about them. They had aired their concerns and come up with solutions to address them. The air had been cleared.

The rest was up to them. Whether they followed through on these actions, I'll never know. As a facilitator, I often wish I could be a fly on the wall in some teams to find out whether they follow through with their commitments to each other.

There's a difference between healthy and unhealthy conflict.

- Unhealthy conflict is usually when the problem at hand hasn't been identified, or there's a lack of self-awareness in admitting to specific issues (e.g., appreciation of different personality types or diversity of working styles between team members), or when a group doesn't come up with any solutions themselves to address things (there's too much of a problem-focus rather than a possibility-focus).
- Healthy conflict, on the other hand, is when the problem is identified, individuals in the group become aware of the dynamics at play, and they actually have autonomy to come up with solutions and actions themselves.

The benefits of healthy conflict include:

- **Stimulating creativity and innovation:** when team members have a safe space to bring their diverse perspectives and ideas to the team, it can lead to creative solutions being developed and critical thinking at its best.

- **Encouraging open communication:** when all team members are comfortable discussing or sharing their differences openly, they're more likely to have strong communication skills and be able to tackle problem-solving and decision-making far more effectively.
- **Strengthening relationships:** when team members successfully resolve conflicts, this builds trust and respect, which leads to developing stronger bonds.
- **Identifying problems early:** conflict can usually be a useful early warning sign, highlighting any issues that need to be resolved.
- **Promoting personal growth:** facing and resolving conflict can be a learning experience for team members, helping them develop better conflict resolution skills and emotional intelligence (and what a useful life skill this is, especially when it's developed in the safe space of a team they work with every day).

How to manage conflict in a team gathering

When you're planning a team gathering, use this checklist below to help guide you with how to best manage conflict that may arise.

☑ **Prepare in advance**

Do your research to help identify any potential reasons of conflict (see list above), and to help you anticipate what might come up during the gathering. If you don't work with or know the team, make sure you have some good pre-gathering conversations with the manager or others in the team to help ascertain these things.

☑ **Create ground rules**:

Plan time during the beginning of your gathering to establish these for your time together – it's great to establish these 'rules' collectively and write them up on the wall (or virtual screen). What does everyone want to get out of the gathering and how do they want to show up, listen to each other, collaborate together? What's acceptable and what's not? This will help bring to the surface any boundaries you'll want to be aware of during your time together.

☑ **Foster open communication**

Encourage active listening among participants (e.g. no interrupting, listening with good intent, encourage team members to provide constructive feedback to one another – avoiding blame games or personal attacks).

☑ **Address any conflict proactively**

If conflict arises, address it as soon as it becomes apparent (don't ignore it!).

☑ **Stay neutral**

As facilitator, it's important to stay neutral and avoid taking any sides – your role is to promote discussion, inclusion, and resolution. This is hard to do if you're an actual team member and you're taking on the role of facilitator (it's often why external facilitators can be really useful resources). Carefully think about how you want to be involved and how you'll involve others.

☑ **Ask open-ended questions**

Help participants express any concerns and viewpoints by asking open-ended questions that promote discussion. It may be a case of taking stock of where you're at and if there's anything people would like to re-commit to for accomplishing in the time you have together.

☑ **Summarise and clarify**

Once people have shared their thoughts and viewpoints, help re-iterate the messages that you've heard and summarise them (this can help clarify any misunderstandings). You might like to generate ideas for solutions together, encouraging team members to generate potential solutions they can think of to a particular issue that arises (then prioritise and decide what solution(s) the team wants to follow through with).

☑ **Stay on track**

Issues of conflict can suck away time from the purpose and focus of the gathering itself. As facilitator, you need to make sure you keep timing on track, don't ignore conflict if it arises, but do make sure you build fat into your agenda so you can make the space to manage any conflict that arises and move on.

The table below outlines the steps I often have in my own head as I'm facilitating a gathering – **listen, observe, reflect, and act**. I find this simple framework helps a team move more swiftly and effectively through any conflict that arises in a team gathering and be able to address smaller issues on the fly. Bigger issues of course may need separate gatherings in themselves – if you need to move on, you may need to remind participants of the purpose of *this* specific gathering and ask them to make sure they follow up on a separate occasion around any specific issues that arise.

Listen-Observe-Reflect-Act

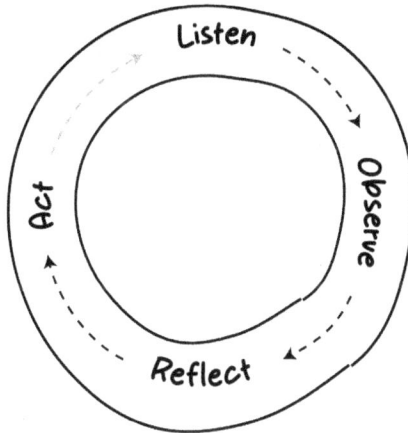

Listen	What might be some of the reasons for the conflict arising (see list above)? If you can identify these before you gather, you'll be at an advantage in the way you plan and design the activities you want to do together as a team.
Observe	What's really going on here? Observe the team in action when they gather. What else are you observing that's going on (things that are said and unsaid)?
Reflect	What will best serve the team, given the outcomes they want to achieve? Are private discussions needed, or collaborative problem-solving collectively as a team?
Act	What follow-up actions do you want to commit to? How will you decide on what these will be?

SECTION 3

Cookie Cutters

Cookie Cutters

Simple tools to shape your gathering

Where to start? A cookie cutter may be all you need to cut through chaos and help to shape your next gathering experience.

HOW TO USE THIS SECTION

This section is designed to inspire you with ideas for elements of your gathering design. If you're not sure where to start, it's sometimes helpful to have a structure to play with. You can sort through the topics below and choose those that are relevant for your team and the situation you find yourselves in.

As you design your gathering time together, always make sure you take account of the 3 P's:

- **Purpose**: Help participants understand why you want them there.
- **Planning**: Design your time together well.
- **Presence**: Meet people where they're at (harness the energy).

By taking heed of these 3Ps, whatever your topic, you're most likely to have a successful gathering as a team.

Each Cookie Cutter section is organised as follows:

- **The problem**, or opportunity, the team has.
- **The outcome** the team wants to achieve.
- A suggested **activity** you can do together as a team.
- Ideas and resources to **go deeper** on this topic.

Each of the Cookie Cutter topics below has downloadable worksheets and resources that you can work on as a team together. You can find these in the resources section of my website.

antoniamilkop.com/resource-download

COOKIE CUTTER 1: WARMING UP

If you want to go fast, go alone. If you want to go far, go together.

- African Proverb

The problem

People will often enter team gatherings from an entirely different context. They might be coming from another meeting, a commute from home or further afield, dropping their kids off at school, or perhaps even coming off the back of a challenging meeting with a stakeholder.

If you don't start your gathering with a good 'warm up', participants are likely to be holding onto thoughts and issues from those previous circumstances they came from. It may be challenging for them to be fully present and attentive to set their minds and focus on the purpose of this team gathering.

The outcome

Warming up well helps set the tone for the rest of your gathering and encourages everyone into a comfortable space. Your aim is to help participants get into the present moment, and become connected and focused on each other.

Great warm up questions help build trust, and develop a safe space for people to share and become more open to dialogue together, enabling them to focus on the purpose ahead – so you can get some great work done in the time you've got together.

Tool - Icebreaker Card Deck

I've developed an Icebreaker Card Deck, suitable for all types of people and groups whether they know each other well already or not. It has been truly tried and tested with many teams I've facilitated gatherings for with lots of success.

People often engage more deeply when they can physically interact with objects. There are numerous neuroscientific reasons why opting for physical objects can be helpful. A deck of cards has the potential to stimulate neuroplasticity in the brain, trigger dopamine release through novelty, and engage diverse brain networks, enabling cognitive flexibility and creative thinking. And it's far more fun and engaging than just a 'warm up question' on a whiteboard.

The questions in the Icebreaker Card Deck are designed to help break the ice, build connections, and engage participants in a collaborative and fun way.

Activity

There are multiple ways to play this game – either as a whole group or in pairs. Feel free to add your own twist to play with the icebreaker questions. My personal favourite is the 'speed dating' method.

1. Print out the cards (one-sided) and cut them up (you can even laminate them if you want). Print multiple copies if you've got a very large group.

2. Give each participant 3 cards each (at random).

3. Ask them to choose *one* card/question that they'd most like to answer (this gives them a choice and encourages divergent thinking).

4. Instruct participants to 'speed date' their way around the group, sharing their answers to the question they've chosen and listening to the other person's answer (two minutes per interaction). You may like

to use a bell or signal to get them to switch over when the time is up and to move on to the next speed date.

5. Carry on the above for as many 'speed dates' as you wish and have time for.

6. Some questions for you (as gathering host) to reflect on after this activity:
   - What did team members find out about each other that they didn't know before?
   - Did you notice any shifts in energy in the group?
   - What difference did this exercise make to the rest of the gathering?

If you're gathering virtually, you can share a selection of the questions via screenshare and ask everyone to choose one to answer in the chat (or via break-out rooms that are switched over every 3 minutes).

Go deeper

You can choose to spend just a few minutes, or a whole hour, on warming up, depending on the team's circumstances and what you feel the team needs. It doesn't *have* to take long. Spending time warming up well will reap benefits in how successful the rest of your gathering is.

There are a variety of other warm up activities you can do as a team (try a simple search on your internet browser, there are so many). Some of my other favourites include:

In-person
   - **People timeline:** asking participants to line themselves up in the order of when they started in the team and/or organisation. Ask the longest standing member to share their words of wisdom to the

rest of the group; and the newest standing member to share their initial insights and any surprises on joining.

- **Photo card decks:** Bring a deck of photos in, spread them out on the floor and ask participants to select an image that captures something about how they feel they're showing up for today. Break out into pairs to discuss with others why they chose this image.

- **Find your pair:** Prepare word pairs on separate pieces of paper (e.g., salt/pepper; sail/wind; black/white; sun/moon; rain/rainbow; ocean/wave; key/lock etc.). Give one word to each participant and have them walk around and asked closed questions (with a yes/no answer) to find out who their pair is. Once they've found their pair, they must learn three new things about each other.

- **One boring fact:** when participants enter the room, ask them to write 'one boring fact' about themselves on a piece of paper, fold it up and put it into a hat. Someone can pick these out at random at intervals throughout the time you have together and play a 'guess who?' game with the group. I've found this activity helps take social pressure off participants to come up with something novel and exciting, as is so often expected in team gatherings.

Virtual

- **Choose an image:** participants choose a background photo, based on a specific theme, and ask them to turn up to the virtual gathering with this set as their background image.

- **Use the 'rename' function** on their name to add/change something to add in about themselves (e.g. their superpower).

- **Online quizzes** (using tools like Menti or Kahoot) are a great way to get a virtual group warmed up and ready for the gathering (they work well with hybrid gatherings too). You might like to base your quiz on the topic or purpose of your day.

- **Emoji check-in:** participants share an emoji or GIF that expresses how they're feeling as they come into the gathering and share this in the chat.
- **Open question:** ask participants to fill in the missing gap of a curiosity-provoking question (that you share in the chat) with their own missing gap. For example, The future is...; Today I'd like to...; Right now, I'd most like to be ...; For breakfast I had...; The shoes I'm wearing are....

> **You can download a free printable worksheet**
> **for this Cookie Cutter at antoniamilkop.com/resource-download**

COOKIE CUTTER 2: MAKING HYBRID WORK FOR US

Think left and think right, and think low and think high.
Oh, the Thinks you can think up if only you try.

- Dr Seuss

The problem

Your team has a mix of those who work remotely and/or in the office. You support flexible work practices in your organisation – hybrid work has lots of advantages, but it also comes with its challenges – decreased collaboration, the ability to 'switch off' when not working, isolation, and less connection to the organisational culture.

You may be trying to figure out how to make hybrid working an effective part of the team's operations. Your current practices are a bit messy and confusing. You realise you're probably not doing the best things to optimise how you work as a collective team.

You don't want to create blanket rules for your team, yet you do want to explore better ways of hybrid working that benefit not only the individuals in the team, but also how you collaborate and operate as a group. You may be struggling to have this conversation at all levels (both within and outside the team).

How might you have this conversation together as a team so that you can explore how you do 'hybrid working' so it works for everyone?

The outcome

The team will:
- Explore different core aspects of hybrid working – identify what's currently working well and what isn't.
- Feel empowered to come up with solutions for how to improve how you best operate as a hybrid team.

- Agree on behaviours that you want to commit to as a team.
- Generate some purposeful ideas or options to experiment with.

Tool - Pre-Survey (before you gather)

Survey each team member before you gather on their perspectives on the questions below (it's best if you can make this an anonymous survey). You can ask them how they feel, say, over the last month.

Score from 1 (low/strongly disagree) to 10 (high/strongly agree):

- **Collaboration**: I have been able to work effectively with my team and other colleagues.
- **Connection**: I am feeling connected to others in my team.
- **Focus and output**: I've been able to focus on work priorities wherever I'm doing my work.
- **Autonomy**: I've been in control over how I do my work, helping me be calm and productive.
- **Mastery**: I've been able to improve at my job by learning more and developing my skills.
- **Purpose**: I feel like I'm part of something important and worthwhile.
- **Life priorities**: my work-life blend is about right.

Collate the aggregate results from the survey and share these with the team.

Activity

1. Use the following discussion questions with your team:
   - What's the data telling us? What have we learned?
   - What's currently working well?
   - What's currently not working so well?

- Where do we want to improve?

2. Generate ideas together as a team that you think will help increase one of the scores from the survey results.
   - What ideas can we generate to potentially try out over the next month?
   - What behaviours would we like to commit to as a team (e.g., what type of work we do in which locations; which collaborative tools we use for which purposes; what days or hours during the working week we're expected to 'be available' for each other as a team)?

3. Try and explore the intersection between 'what **I** need' and 'what **we** need as a team' and 'what the **organisation** needs'. This is where you'll find some gems for action.
   - How might we put our chosen idea(s) into action (what, when, who, and how)? Who else do we need to involve?

Go deeper

The book *Flexperts, by Gillian Brookes* (https://www.gillianbrookes. co.nz/shop/flexperts) is a must-read for anyone considering how to get the best from flex in a world that's ever changing. It's full of useful tools and templates, which have been tried and tested across multiple industries. Based in New Zealand, Gillian also provides useful workshops and other services, which support leaders and organisations evolve and develop their flex strategies enabling them to keep up to date with the ever-changing world.

> **You can download a free printable worksheet for this Cookie Cutter at antoniamilkop.com/resource-download**

COOKIE CUTTER 3: PLAYING TO OUR STRENGTHS

Everybody is a genius. But if you judge a fish by its ability to climb a tree, it will live its whole life believing that it is stupid.

- Unknown

The problem

Lots of teams work together without really knowing what make each person operate at their best (or worst). Teams go from day-to-day without asking some very simple questions that could help them fine-tune how they best operate together as a team and their preferred ways of working and combining their working styles together. They haven't yet discovered what their team members might be naturally talented in, or what they might be able to offer to them.

Teams thrive when there's recognition from the leaders that each person in the team has different talents, and the individual contributors in a team appreciate these different talents in each other. No one individual has all the talents. When you can target who does what, applying each individual's natural talents in specific ways, and leverage ways in which people work best together, a team will function at its best. Often stress points between people are signs of misunderstood talents.

For example, I once had a colleague who I thought always seemed to block my ability to get stuff done – they kept wanting to think more deeply about it, hold the delivery, delay the timeframe, and instead have more conversations together before we could get going on something. Whereas I felt we had enough information and could just go ahead and get on with it! Had I better understood that this person's talents were to obtain a depth and breadth of understanding and input before they approached a task, as well as assessing all the risks involved, I probably would have felt more patient with them during their continued exploration. I would have better appreciated the depth of wisdom that they brought to the task at hand so that we could make sure we got the *right* result, not just any result.

The outcome

Team members will:

- Build awareness of what brings out the best and worst in each other.
- Gain appreciation of the ways in which other team members operate and their preferred styles of working.
- Discover ways in which to apply their strengths in the team, in knowing what they can offer to others, and what help they can ask from others.

They'll explore, appreciate, and purposefully apply their different strengths, building a foundation of open communication and mutual respect for different ways of working and styles among the team.

Tool – Stronger Together Matrix

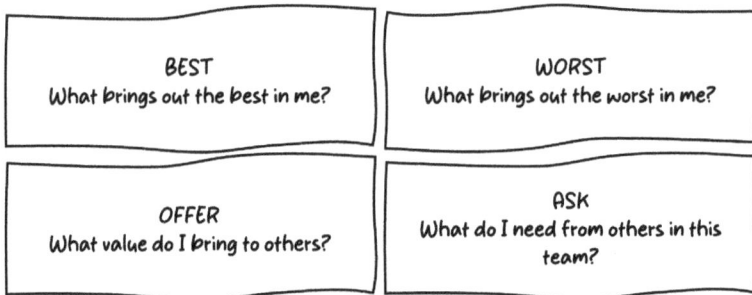

BEST What brings out the best in me?	WORST What brings out the worst in me?
OFFER What value do I bring to others?	ASK What do I need from others in this team?

Activity

1. **Draw** up the quadrant and questions above on large flipchart paper *(or an online whiteboard if you're meeting virtually)*.

2. **Ask** each team member to answer each of the four questions (one post-it note per person per quadrant). Try and encourage participants to be as specific as possible in their answers (avoid vague statements). Make sure everyone writes their name or initials on each post-it note they write.

3. **Discuss** each other's answers together as a team. You may notice patterns, commonalities, and/or differences amongst team members. Use the following questions to help guide your discussion:

    - What insights have you gained about yourself and/or your colleagues during this activity?
    - Is there anything that surprises you?
    - Can you see combinations of talents in different people that might complement one another? Where two or three people working together could create a better whole?
    - Are there any obvious themes that emerge for us as a collective team?
    - Are there any actions we want to follow up with as a result?

Go deeper

For individuals who have done a CliftonStrengths®[13] assessment, you can use your strengths profiles to help expand with more specificity and nuance around the answers above (i.e. 'Bring/Need' resource for OFFER/ASK questions; and the 'Personal Insights' resource for BEST/ WORST questions).

If your team members don't already have a CliftonStrengths® profile, you may like to get them to individually answer the following questions around the 5Es exercise to help them self-diagnose and discover a bit more about their natural talents:

- Ease: what comes easily or naturally for you?

- Enthusiasm: what do you look forward to?
- Excellence: what has been third party validated by others?
- Energy: what lights you up?
- Engagement: what will you push yourself beyond challenges for?

If you're a team that already knows your CliftonStrengths® profiles, check out the other resources available on my website (antoniamilkop. com/resources), which have a variety of other tools and activities you may like to experiment with as a team.

You can download a free printable worksheet for this Cookie Cutter at antoniamilkop.com/resource-download

---

COOKIE CUTTER 4: ARTICULATING OUR PURPOSE

A man without a purpose is like a ship without a rudder.

- Thomas Carlyle

The problem

Everyone in the team knows *what* you do and *how* you do it, but they can't clearly articulate *why* you exist as a team – what your higher purpose, or cause, actually is. Team members may know intrinsically what the purpose of the team is, but when asked to explain this out loud, they all provide very different answers. If your team can't explain its purpose to themselves, how is anyone else you work with going to understand why you do what you do?

The outcome

'Why' is what gets us out of bed in the morning – creating a memorable purpose statement that describes why your team exists helps you not only feel more motivated and aligned with what you're all doing at work, but it also helps you clearly explain to others the reason that you exist.

As a team:

- You'll discuss the purpose (the 'why') of your team and explore differences in opinions and expressions of what this is.
- Create statements that help the team clearly express their purpose as a team – both to yourselves as well as your stakeholders.
- Agree on a final purpose statement that best describes why you do what you do, aligns well with your organisational purpose, and can be used in communication with others.

Tool 1 - Simon Sinek's Golden Circle

If you haven't already heard of Simon Sinek's 'Golden Circle' (simon-sinek.com/golden-circle), get familiar with it.[14]

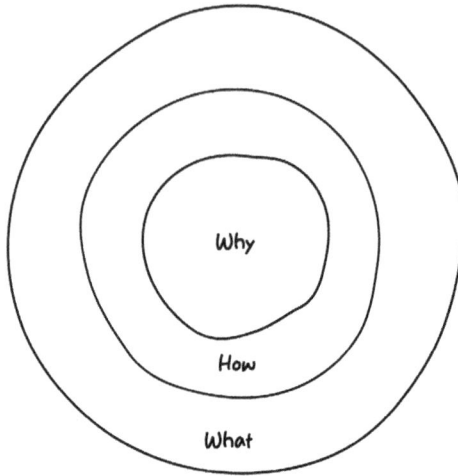

His famous TED talk[15] reached millions of views and is a great, easy-to-follow, and short explanation of why clearly articulating 'the why' is so important.

> *The inspired leaders—every single one of them, regardless of their industry—think, act, and communicate from the inside out. People don't buy WHAT you do, they buy WHY you do it.*
>
> - Simon Sinek

Tool 2 – Good versus Poor Purpose Statements

A GOOD STATEMENT	A POOR STATEMENT
Uses language your stakeholders use	Uses jargon your audience doesn't understand
Is emotionally stirring	Is logical and cold
Communicates the 'why'	Communicates only the 'what' or 'how'
Is concise	Is long
Is a single, powerful sentence	Is a rambling paragraph
Sounds good said out loud	Is hard to say out loud
Is memorable	Is forgettable
Surprises	Is dull
Is actionable	Can't be quantified
Is specific	Is vague

Activity

1. Discuss together your personal reflections on Simon Sinek's Golden Circle after watching the TED talk.

2. Find examples of purpose statements from others that inspire you and others that you think are a bit rubbish (you can research ones via company websites, annual reports etc.). Discuss what you think makes

some of these purpose statements sing and others sink? You may wish to use the 'good vs. poor' table to help guide this discussion.

3. Split the group into smaller groups of 3-4 people each. Discuss the following questions together:
    - What gets you out of bed in the morning to come to work?
    - What are we here to contribute?
    - What challenges are we trying to overcome?
    - What opportunities are we trying to embrace?
    - How would we like our work to be remembered in 100 years' time?

4. Provide each small group with some index cards and ask them to come up with their answers to the following (they can write more than one index card if they like):
    - We are here to... *(desired impact)*
    - By... *(how we do it uniquely)*
    - For the good of... *(who we serve)*.

5. Each small group can then share back to the larger group the draft purpose statements they've come up with so far.

6. For each of the index cards, ask the whole team to score using the 'good vs. poor' criteria in the table above.

7. Discuss the highest scores and come up with a team purpose statement you all agree on. (If you need to do more work to refine it, that's fine – work out what aspects need more work and who can follow up).

Go deeper

As a team, discuss together what you think makes a good purpose statement. Have a look at the 11 purpose statements below and see if you can
guess who they're from.

> ## Who do these purpose statements belong to?
>
> Can you guess which organisations these purpose statements
> belong to (answers in footnotes!).
>
> 1. *To grow New Zealand for all*
> 2. *To entertain, inform and inspire people around the globe
>   through the power of unparalleled storytelling, reflecting the
>   iconic brands, creative minds and innovative technologies
>   that make ours the world's premier entertainment company.*
> 3. *A more liveable, green and people friendly future.*
> 4. *We want to entertain the world. Whatever your taste, and no
>   matter where you live, we give you access to best-in-class TV
>   series, documentaries, feature films and games.*
> 5. *To inspire and nurture the human spirit – one person, one
>   cup and one neighborhood at a time.*
> 6. *Wellington is a lively city with a thriving cultural life, talented
>   people, and cutting-edge businesses.*
> 7. *Our purpose is to advance an ambitious, resilient and well-
>   governed New Zealand.*
> 8. *We act in the world to build a safer, more prosperous and
>   more sustainable future for New Zealanders.*
> 9. *We are the Government's primary adviser on environmental
>   matters. We also have a stewardship role. This involves*

taking a long-term perspective on environmental issues when making decisions.

10. To grow companies internationally – bigger, better, faster – for the good of NZ.

11. To organise the world's information and make it universally accessible and useful.

Answers: 1. NZ Ministry of Business, Innovation & Employment, **2.** Disney, **3.** Auckland Council, **4.** Netflix, **5.** Starbucks, **6.** Wellington City Council, **7.** NZ Department of the Prime Minister and Cabinet, **8.** NZ Foreign Affairs and Trade, **9.** NZ Ministry for the Environment, **10.** NZ Trade & Enterprise, **11.** Google.

You can download a free printable worksheet for this Cookie Cutter at antoniamilkop.com/resource-download

COOKIE CUTTER 5: CRAFTING A TEAM VISION

Vision is the art of seeing what is invisible to others.

- Jonathan Swift

The problem

Maybe you have a vision statement as an organisation. It might feel inspiring, but it's quite lofty and not very directionally focused on your team's role and purpose. If you could articulate a vision for your team, you'd be able to better know what direction you're going in and steer in a clear course towards that vision and, at the same time, bring others along on the journey with you.

The outcome

In this gathering, you will collectively create a draft team vision statement, which you can later refine and test with others. This vision statement will define where you, as a team, aspire to be (the future state).

The team will:

- Understand the difference between purpose, mission, and vision.
- Recognise the importance of a shared team vision to drive towards your goals, outcomes, and desired future state.
- Be able to describe something potentially 'abstract' to others (e.g. key partners, stakeholders, clients) in a way that's memorable, compelling, and easily understood by others.

Tool – The 3Cs (Clarity, Conviction, Connection)

Clarity – are we clear in what we see?

Conviction – can we easily describe a desired future state to others and do we believe in it ourselves?

Connection – what's our role in it all? How do we bring others along?

Activity

1. Describe the difference between purpose, mission, and vision (these are often misunderstood).
    - **Purpose:** describes the 'why' in what you do (a pre-requisite for this gathering).
    - **Mission:** actionable vision statement – it's something that gives the 'how' to your vision. In other words, it's your work programme showing the specifics on *how* you will achieve your goals, outcomes, and desired future state.
    - **Vision:** doesn't just describe where you want to be in the world, but where you want the world to be because of you. It's meant to be inspiring, aspirational, motivating, and something that will last into the future.

2. Reflect on your organisation's purpose, mission, and vision statements, if you have them. Discuss your thoughts together as a team on how your vision statement meets the 3C questions above around Clarity, Conviction, and Connection. What are your thoughts?

3. Provide everyone with some creative materials (e.g. LEGO, A3 paper and colouring pens, photo cards, magazines – anything that helps them to be creative).
    - Ask everyone to individually build/draw/create something that describes their desired future state for the team, using the following questions as prompts (no descriptive words are allowed at this stage – it has to be visual only):
        a. What does the future look and feel like for this team?

    b. What are some experiences we'd be having if we realised our vision?

- Once you've built/drawn/created something visual, now add 1-5 descriptive words to this visual creation – share these words as a team together.

4. In smaller groups, using your descriptive words, craft one or two vision statements that build on these descriptions. Share these together as a team. Often vision statements are written in the present tense (describing a future state) and start with adverbs like:
   - Inspiring...
   - Creating...
   - Making...
   - We are....
   - Some vision statements are phrased as questions, e.g. 'What if...?'. A question can be a useful way to phrase a vision statement as it's something a team can easily check in with over time and assess how they are working towards this aspirational future state.

5. Refining your vision statement: using the draft statements created by the small groups, discuss together as a team on what you like and don't like, and craft a collective vision statement for your team that you can all agree on.
   - How does it stack up against the 3Cs – Clarity, Conviction, Connection?
   - Does your vision describe a future state and direction?
   - Is it easily understood by others?
   - Does it engage hearts and minds?
   - Does it avoid timeframes?

Go deeper

Test your vision statement with others you work with – colleagues, stakeholders, and partners. You may like to run specific gatherings or 'drop in' sessions for these groups so you can socialise your team's vision, receive feedback, get buy-in where it's needed and hopefully discover relevant connection points for your team's future direction.

> **You can download a free printable worksheet for this Cookie Cutter at antoniamilkop.com/resource-download**

COOKIE CUTTER 6: CREATING AN ELEVATOR PITCH

Simplicity is the ultimate sophistication.

- attributed to Leonardo da Vinci

The problem

Team members will often know exactly what they do for their job, why their team exists and the direction their team is going in (especially if they've done the purpose and vision work above!). But they might be rubbish at communicating this to others. If your team isn't clearly singing from the same song sheet (i.e., sharing similar messages about your why, what, and where to as a team and the role they play in this), you'll find others will be confused about when they can and should interact with your team and how to do so.

The outcome

When confronted with a question like 'what do you do?' or 'tell me about yourself', team members will be prepared to answer these questions with a pithy summary that feels authentic to them. Also, team members will share consistent messages to others – not a bunch of disparate and confusing ones – meaning you're communicating a clear and compelling story to others.

Your team will be able to clearly articulate their own elevator pitch – a short, personalised, interesting, and compelling summary of what the team's about and the role they play in that. An elevator pitch can be delivered in a short amount of time (e.g., the time it takes to ride a few floors in an elevator), the goal being to capture the listener's attention, communicate key information and leave a lasting impression. It's a clear, engaging summary and delivered in a way that sparks interest, making the listener want to learn more.

Tool – Crafting Questions

Who are you?

- Your name and team.

What do you do?

- What your specific role is in the team and the differentiator or uniqueness you bring.

Why does it matter?

- Are there specific problems you're solving, or benefits you bring to others? What are these? Help the audience understand the relevant and importance of your work.

What's the call to action?

- Conclude your pitch by sharing what you're seeking from the person you're sharing with – is it information, investment, partnerships, or something else? Make it clear about what action or response you hope to generate.

Activity

1. **Before the gathering:**
   - This can be a fun activity to 'test out' amongst team members first – just tell them you're taking them on a short elevator ride to ask them a question, which they have to answer in the duration you're in the elevator – ideally this is no longer than 45 seconds in length. Ask them: 'What do you do?' Record their answers. Time them and cut them off if they go over 45 seconds – that's all they'll get.
   - Collate all team member's answers together in one place.

2. During the gathering:

- If required, you may like to recap with the team your purpose and vision. Share back the collated answers from team members from the elevator pitch. How consistent or different were the different responses everyone gave? You can discuss and explore the various answers. What stands out? What's missing? How clear, compelling, and interesting were each of the answers?
- Ask each team member to re-develop their own elevator pitch, one that feels authentic to them, and can be delivered in a way, or style, that they can confidentially express to others and feel comfortable with. They may like to do this as individuals or in pairs.
- As a team, use the crafting questions above and ask them to improve their own elevator pitch, then practice these out on each other.

3. After the gathering:

- Test this out on others when you're next in an elevator or at a networking event. What do you notice as a result?

Go deeper

When you go along to a meeting, how do you explain what your team does to others? Continue to practice your elevator pitches – in your team, with other colleagues, or in meetings you go to. Explaining your role and your message to others is all part of effective communication and the art of storytelling – and differentiating what the audience in question is most interested to hear about.

When you're testing your elevator pitch/es with others, notice the responses you get. Does the call to action follow up you had hoped for happen as a result? If not, what extra tweaks or internal/external communications might you consider to successfully convey messages about who you are and what you do?

COOKIE CUTTER 7: LIVING OUR TEAM'S VALUES

True strength lies in our ability to embrace vulnerability,
live in alignment with our deepest values,
and cultivate the courage to stand wholeheartedly in our truth.

- Brené Brown

The problem

Every individual has different belief systems and principles that they use to guide and shape their behaviour and decision-making. It's important that team members have a shared understanding of each other's values and how these align with the collective team, or organisational values. When values are mis-aligned, it leads to misunderstandings, poor communication and collaboration, a lack of team cohesion, inconsistent decision-making, and decreased morale and motivation, and interpersonal conflict due to a lack of understanding or respect for diverse perspectives.

Values

Values play a significant role in shaping a person's identity and worldview. Some values may be non-negotiable for people, and others may be more flexible and subject to change over time. Teams are made up of different individuals – when groups hold different values, it can lead to conflicts and misunderstandings – so it's important to understand other people's values in your team. Don't mistake values as being preferences, or universal things that can apply to everyone (which is often the case if 'organisational values'are imposed on a diverse range of people, without them figuring out their own individual values first and how these align to others).

The outcome

This exercises will help team members identify their own personal values, articulate why these are important to them, and how they influence their decisions. They'll be able to better identify alignments or conflicts between differing values and identify steps to take about how to effectively navigate through these.

Each team member will:

- Identify values that are most important to them and others in the team, and why.
- Explore how values align to their work and what may be in conflict for them (and approaches to overcome this).
- Map how their own individual values align with the team's and/or organisational values.

Tool – Values Card Sort Activity

You can print out an easy-to-use downloadable card sort activity from the resources library on my website (antoniamilkop.com/resources). Print multiple copies and cut up the pages into 'cards' (one document/pack per person or small group).

Activity

1. Ask each individual to sort through the list of values card into piles:
   - Very important to me
   - Sometimes important to me
   - Not of importance to me.

2. Prioritise the 'Very important to me' pile into your Top 5 (in order of importance to you). Discuss together in pairs why you chose these ones, using the following questions as prompts:
   - What do I care most about in life right now? Why is that?

- How do the people I spend the most time with reflect these values?
- Which of my values is conflicted right now? What do I need to do about this conflict?

3. Ask each individual to write down the top two values from their individual lists (one value per post it note). Post these up on a wall (or electronic whiteboard or word cloud). Discuss as a team, using the following questions as prompts:
   - What motivates us?
   - What guides our decisions?
   - What are our commonalities or differences in the way we filter (values)?
   - How do our strengths align with our values?
   - What are our current challenges? What might they be in the future?

Go deeper

Check in regularly with yourself and your team members on how they are 'walking the talk' with their core values.

- What are some behaviours that are supporting your values?
- What are some behaviours that appear to be outside of your values?
- Can you think of some recent examples of when you were fully living in your values?
- What are some ways you can check in on yourself as to how you're walking the talk with your values?
- Who is someone that supports your efforts to live in your values? What does support from this person look like?

COOKIE CUTTER 8: DEFINING SUCCESS

Unity is strength. When there is teamwork and collaboration, wonderful things can be achieved.

- Mattie Stepanek

The problem

If you don't know what success looks like for you collectively as a team, you'll lack direction as a team. Individuals will be more likely to work towards their individual goals and may struggle to find purpose and motivation when they don't have a clear steer of what they are working collectively towards. Inconsistencies will result and projects will lack effective coordination and result in misalignment as a team, with potential confusion and misunderstanding as a team regarding roles, responsibilities, and expectations.

The outcome

This activity provides some instructions for how you can break down goals and socialise these together as a team, to enable constructive conversations so your team can align itself to 'what success looks like' and travel towards it. Team members will come away with a collective understanding of what success looks and feels like as a team and how to move in that direction.

You will:

- Identify what success looks like for:
  - me as an individual
  - the team
  - the organisation
  - our customers/stakeholders (i.e., the people we serve).

- Understand the impact of what success means for the team.
- Develop goals aligned to your business plan.
- Choose priority focus areas for a time period (for you to define).

Tool – Reflection Questions

This activity uses a series of reflective questions to guide individual and team discussion.

Activity

1. **Pre-gathering**: ask individuals in the team to reflect on the following questions before you gather together as a team. Identify the time period you want to focus your 'success criteria' on (for example, the next quarter).
   - What does success look and feel like for YOU over the next quarter?
   - What does it look like for our stakeholders/customers (people we serve) over the next quarter?
   - What does it look like for our team?
   - What does it look like for our organisation/our country/our world?

2. **During team gathering:**
   - **Scene setting** by bringing along any collateral that will be useful for defining success as a team. Re-familiarise yourself with the team's work objectives, goals, or business plan.
   - **Share back** your individual answers from the pre-gathering questions collectively as a team and discuss your answers (it's great if you can make these visual on a wall somewhere).
   - **Reflect on** the following questions:

- What do we expect to see happen as a result of what we've defined as success?
- What do we believe is possible?
- What goals can we set as a team (make these SMART goals)?
- Out of the list of goals we've identified, which are most important to realising success? (you may like to use something like dot stickers to vote collectively on the full list)?
- Decide on 1-3 goals per month to focus our collective effort on as a team over the next quarter (or whatever time period you have defined). These will be what you choose to focus your effort on as being the top priorities to realise success as a team.

Go deeper

1. If you have quarterly planning days as a team, invite your key partners, customers, or stakeholders to join in for part of it and give their feedback and suggestions on how you're going on your success criteria as a team. What improvements can be made? How so? What's been working well and what hasn't?

2. The MoSCoW prioritisation tool (created by Dai Clegg of Oracle® UK Consulting in the mid-1990s) is a useful approach for teams to use to help sort tasks into critical and non-critical categories. Most teams I meet have more than enough on their plates, and their struggles lie in figuring out just how to prioritise the list of many tasks they must achieve with capacity and resources that they have.
   - **Must-haves**: What are the things we must do?
   - **Should-haves**: What do we consider important, but not vital?
   - **Could-haves**: What are some 'nice to haves'?

- **Won't haves**: What do we want to drop as it won't add value or have much impact?

3. The 4Ds framework (Delete, Delegate, Defer, Do) is another activity you can use in teams, especially when there's varying level of work constraints amongst team members, and they're trying to figure out how to share the workload between themselves and/or others.
   - **Delete**: there's no huge risk or downside of not doing this task
   - **Delegate**: it's not necessarily something that depends on your skillset
   - **Defer**: If you can't delete it
   - **Do**: Only you can do this

> **You can download a free printable worksheet for this Cookie Cutter at antoniamilkop.com/resource-download**

COOKIE CUTTER 9: SETTING OUR GATHERING RHYTHMS

> *Team rhythms are the heartbeat of collaboration,*
> *the cadence of unity, and the melody of success.*

The problem

If you're a manager and you don't plan in advance why, when, and how you want to gather your team, you'll find a year whizzes by and you won't have accomplished what you set out to do. You will miss valuable opportunities to help keep the work on-track, sustain workloads across the team, make timely decisions, and ensure that everyone is singing to the same song sheet.

The outcome

This activity helps you acknowledge and define what gathering rhythms work best for you as a team to bring out the best in everyone. High performing teams spend a lot of time together, so if you intentionally plan ahead of time, you can design a rhythm for your team that is fit-for-purpose and meets your goals, time, constraints, and budgets.

Tool – Rhythms Template

Have a go at filling in your intentions for the year ahead, including things you already know are happening. For inspiration, you can use the template example provided earlier in Section 2 on Planning – Questions to consider.

Gathering Purpose	Frequency	Delivery Mode	Commitments
The 'why' you're gathering	Daily, weekly, quarterly etc.?	In-person, virtual or hybrid?	What do you intend to commit to as a result of this gathering?

Activity

1. **Before the year starts**: complete this template of your intentions around how you want your team to gather.

2. **Discuss the following with your team:**
   - What's missing?
   - What existing rhythms do we already have in place? (e.g., governance/decision points, planning cadences, financial, personal). And what frequency do these occur (i.e. daily, weekly, monthly, quarterly, annual)?
   - What's currently working well? (Keep)
   - What's currently not working well? (Stop)
   - Is there anything new we want to introduce (Start).

Go deeper

Make sure to follow through with any commitments you make to keep, stop, and start new things. At regular intervals throughout the year, assess what's working and what's not, where value is being added and outcomes are being met. Be prepared to flex and evolve your team rhythms as things change (as they inevitably always do).

You can download a free printable worksheet for this Cookie Cutter at antoniamilkop.com/resource-download

---

COOKIE CUTTER 10: LOOKING BACK TO MOVE FORWARD

Ka mua, ka muri.
(Walking backwards into the future.)

- a Māori proverb

The problem

Hindsight is great form of wisdom. When we don't take stock and learn from the past, we often repeat similar mistakes without the insight to know how to adapt or change moving forward. If you don't take the time to focus on and learn from the past, you may find yourself drifting aimlessly as a team. Much like a well-seasoned recipe, reflection is the spice of progress.

The outcome

As a result of this activity, your team will be able to:

- Celebrate achievements and things that went well
- Reflect on things that were lacking or made work life difficult
- Capture key takeaways and lessons to learn from
- Express ideas for improvements using discussion, insights, and wisdom for how you best move forward as a team.

Tool – Retro Templates

There are many retro templates to choose from, I'm a fan of the 4Ls retro approach (Love, Long, Loathe, Learn). Not only do a team reflect as individuals, but also as a group. You can download a template for a retro from the resources library of my website (antoniamilkop.com/resources).

Activity

1. **Reflect**: looking back on your past week (or chosen timeframe), use the 4Ls template, asking each team member to contribute at least one post-it note in each of the sections. You can either do this in-person using flipchart/post-its, or via virtual whiteboard. What do you observe? Celebrate successes together, discuss any key themes that are emerging, or maybe particular pain points you've had as a team.

2. **Improve**: In each of the columns, add ideas for improvements to take on the next week (or chosen timeframe).

3. **Action**: prioritise your 'ideas for improvement' to a shorter list of perhaps two or three that you wish to follow up with as a team.

Go deeper

If you want to scale this activity up to focus with a more longer-term lens, use the 4Ls template above and also discuss the following as a team:

- How did we define success at the beginning? Where are we now?
- If you're a larger group (e.g., branch or organisation-wide), **before you gather**, ask each sub-team to create a large flipchart for their team (encourage them to be as creative as they like), outlining:
  - Celebrating successes: What do we see as our greatest achievements over the last [time period]? What's been going well? What do we feel most proud of?
  - Challenges: What have been some of the barriers or obstacles that have gotten in our way? What do we think was missing?
  - Surprises: What's happened that we didn't expect?
  - Insights: What have we learned?
- Hopes and aspirations for next [time period]? **When you gather**, each sub-team can review each other's flipcharts and celebrate each other's successes and learnings.

- Break out into small groups and do a magic wand exercise – 'if I could wave a magic wand...':
  - What would you like to see happen next quarter/year (wildest dreams)?
  - What would this magic wand enable you to do?
  - What's needed to make these things happen (be realistic and ambitious)?
  - What might be holding you back?
  - How might you make these things a reality?
  - What support would you need?
- Agree to commit to some actions or follow-ups as a result of your discussion.

You can download a free printable worksheet for this Cookie Cutter at antoniamilkop.com/resource-download

SECTION 4

Wrapping Up

Wrapping Up

No one is born a great cook, one learns by doing.

- Julia Child

I hope that the ideas in this book resonate strongly with you and that you're now feeling inspired to experiment with some new ways of facilitating your own team gatherings.

Team gatherings are an integral part of the maintenance and hygiene that's needed for a healthy team to function well and perform at its best. If teams don't gather purposefully, you're going to become disconnected and less engaged.

Successful teams spend a lot of time together, and great team gatherings don't just happen by chance. Purposeful design beforehand saves you time in the long run and will lead to better results for you and your team.

If you're a manager or leader of a team, don't underestimate how important your role is in initiating, coordinating, and orchestrating the cadences and rhythms for your team's gatherings. Team members *want* to have trust and confidence in you. An obvious way of building and growing this is through connection and collaboration. Planning and orchestrating a rhythm of team gatherings throughout the year, all of which have specific purposes and intended results, will be so worth your investment in time and energy. It'll mean you're not only investing in your team and its growth, but you're also investing in your own leadership growth, stability of the team, and their confidence in you as their leader.

If you're a facilitator, I hope that reading the ideas in this book has inspired you to try out some new things when you're next facilitating a team gathering.

The 3Ps of purposeful team gatherings

If there's only one thing you remember from this book, remember the 3Ps, and why you must consider all three (P^3) together.

- **Purpose**: Help participants understand why you want them there.
- **Planning**: Design your time together well.
- **Presence**: Meet people where they're at (harness the energy).

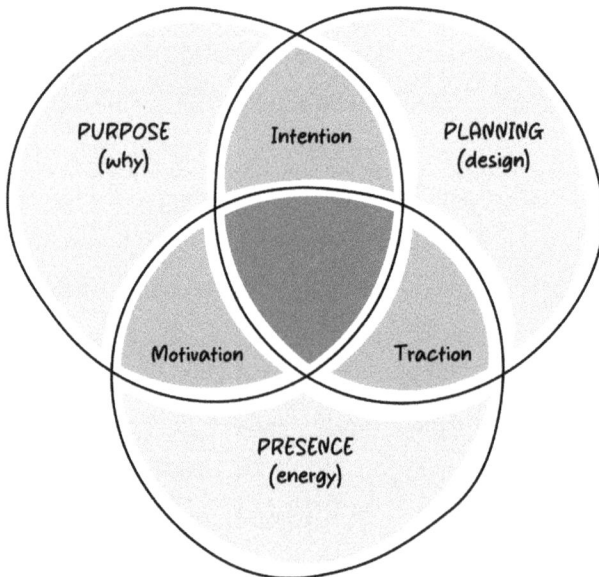

If you keep these three essential ingredients in mind every time you're organising, attending, or facilitating a team gathering, you'll experience a significant boost in the overall success of how your gatherings go.

- **Purpose + Planning** creates *intention*. Participants know why they're turning up and what's expected of them and others.
- **Planning + Presence** creates *traction*. Participants are engaged and willing to participate and make stuff happen – before, during, and after the gathering.
- **Presence + Purpose** creates *motivation*. People know why they're there and how they're showing up. They're inspired to take part.

When you're missing one of these essential three ingredients you may find:

- *Without purpose* - your planning will be time-consuming and probably miss the mark.
- *Without planning* - you risk not covering all that you need to in the time that you have or are able to prepare for unforeseen eventualities (they're likely to happen).
- *Without presence* - you're missing the connection between yourself as facilitator and who's participating to ensure you engage who they are and why they're there.

Cookie Cutter topics

The small selection of Cookie Cutter topics provided in this book draw on some popular activities that I've used successfully in my facilitation work. My hope is that you'll be able to use these and adapt them to your own purposes. I'd love to hear from you about what's worked for you, and what hasn't.

You can download useful resources, including worksheets and tools explored in this book (plus more!) from the resources library on my website:

antoniamilkop.com/resource-download

LET'S STAY IN TOUCH

I'd love to stay connected and hear any feedback you have on this book, or any stories you wish to share about how you get along with hosting your own team gatherings.

- Subscribe to Antonia's newsletter: antoniamilkop.com/contact
- Connect with Antonia on LinkedIn: linkedin.com/in/ antonia-milkop

You are always welcome to get in touch.

WORK WITH ANTONIA MILKOP

If you put into practice all the ideas and suggestions covered in this book, you probably won't need much help to facilitate your team gatherings! However, there are always times when an external pair of hands is very helpful and required, so do reach out to Antonia if you'd like her support with your team.

Antonia also provides a range of other services for leaders and teams, so if you want to grow your impact and performance (for yourself or for you team), it would be her privilege to guide you on whatever journey you may find yourself on. Many of these services can be provided either in-person or virtually.

Facilitation

Antonia's mission is to ignite potential in teams and help them make more of a positive impact in the work they do. Antonia can support you in planning, designing, and facilitating your team gatherings, and discuss the purpose and intended outcomes you are wanting to achieve.

Leadership coaching

Coaching is an effective and powerful opportunity to enhance your potential, your leadership, your impact, and your performance. Antonia's work with high-performing leaders and managers helps them find a safe and trusted space to authentically grow in their own thinking.

Antonia tailors her one-on-one coaching packages to an individual's personal goals and needs, supporting them work through challenges and how to overcome these. She acts as a catalyst to help ignite untapped potential, helps build your confidence, and supports you in navigating your own pathway forward.

Antonia has been a Gallup-Certified Strengths Coach since 2018. She is a member of the International Coaching Federation (ICF) and holds her Professional Certified Coach (PCC) accreditation with the ICF.

Keynote speaking

Antonia is available for keynote speaking on *Mahi-Tahi for Teams* (helping teams work better together), as well as other topics. Please contact Antonia for more information.

Team strengths-based coaching

Antonia provides strengths-based coaching and facilitation for teams and supports individuals to build awareness of their unique talents. Using the CliftonStrengths® framework, each team member grows self-awareness and appreciation of their own unique strengths as well as the strengths of others they work with. Teams discover a 'common language' they can use that's positively framed (but doesn't ignore weakness or growth areas). Teams explore partnerships between different individuals in a team and how they can best work together based on their strengths.

Antonia creates a safe, trusted, and fun environment where your team can amplify the way you work together, talk through challenges more easily, and work through ways to overcome them. Antonia is a certified Gallup® Global Strengths Coach and specialises in coaching teams around their strengths.

Facilitation mentoring

If you're wanting to upskill your facilitation skills, and grow in confidence to deliver gatherings, Antonia provides useful mentoring support to those looking to enhance their own facilitation skills. Areas include developing specific skills, guidance and help on the planning process, problem-solving support, honest feedback and reflection, shadowing, building confidence, and the sharing of helpful resources.

Online courses

If you're interested in a training course with Antonia on how to host purposeful team gatherings, please contact Antonia for more information.

Acknowledgements

I'm immensely grateful to all the individuals and teams who have helped contribute to the creation of the content in this book. Their inspiration, encouragement, experience, and case studies have been invaluable to me to put these tools and methods into practice and experiment with them.

Thank you to all you wonderful readers for reading this book, I appreciate you! Please do share any insights you've got from this book with others, and experiment with designing and delivering your team gathering with a more purposeful twist.

My deepest gratitude goes towards my coach and mentor (and unbelievable cheerleader), Christopher Miller (christophermiller.co.nz), in helping me believe in myself and get over any imposter syndrome I had about authoring, and just to start somewhere – share the wisdom and experiences I've had and believing that its result will be valuable for others. I found the more I wrote, the more fun I had putting my ideas and experience on to paper.

My support crew has been many, you know who you are, and I am so grateful to you all! Especially those of you who have trawled through the pages of this book in its first iterations, tested ideas with me, been guinea pigs for cookie cutters, and provided constructive feedback to keep me on track and produce something that's solid, and the many sound boarding conversations or emails, which have helped expand my thinking and put it on the page.

A special thanks to my friend and client, Lisa Docherty, who happens to have been a freelance editor in a previous life and is now a manager in the public sector. Lisa has been there for me throughout this whole journey of writing, especially when I was having wobbly moments in France. She is also the person I have channelled most when writing to ensure what I write is relevant to the mindset of a busy manager, with lots on their plate in both work and life.

I'm very grateful for the final proofreaders – Lisa Docherty, Paul Ramsay (aka 'Red Pen Ramsay' in his workplace!), and my wonderful husband, Ashley Milkop. Thanks for your discerning eyes catching out those stray commas, grammatical errors, and font whoopsies.

I've been fortunate to have some incredibly supportive managers throughout my career – you have all inspired, enabled and motivated me. I hope this book is relevant, practical, and useful for you – it's one that can be easily skim-read or dipped into for inspiration or plunged into in great depth.

To my beloved husband and children, thank you for your belief in me, and your patience and understanding during the many hours I've spent researching and writing. Your love has been my anchor, and I consider myself incredibly fortunate to have you in my life. I am particularly grateful for my husband's discerning insight, his constructive and direct feedback, accompanied by instances of genuine admiration and a delightful touch of "wow, this is really impressive!" (words of affirmation do not come lightly to him).

And lastly, a huge thank you to my publisher, Hambone Publishing (hambonepublishing.com.au), for supporting me throughout this writing journey. Mish, Ben and the team – you've been a phenomenal support and have always been there for me when I've got stuck and needed a bit of sound boarding to help me move forward! Thank you all those that have been involved in the production and publication process, making it fun and helping me achieve something I've never done before.

This book would not have been possible without the collective efforts of these wonderful individuals, and for that, I am truly thankful.

References

BOOKS THAT HAVE INSPIRED ME

- *Four Thousand Weeks – Time Management for Mortals.* Oliver Burkeman (2022)
- *The Five Dysfunctions of a Team. A Leadership Fable.* Patrick Lencioni (2002)
- *The 6 Types of Working Genius. A Better Way to Understand Your Gifts, Your Frustrations, and Your Team.* Patrick Lencioni (2022)
- *The Art of Deliberate Success. The 10 Behaviours of Successful People.* David Keane (2012)
- *The Art of Gathering.* How We Meet and Why It Matters. Priya Parker (2019)
- *Atlas of the Heart. Mapping Meaningful Connection and the Language of Human Experience.* Brené Brown (2021)
- *Atomic Habits: An Easy & Proven Way to Build Good Habits & Break Bad Ones.* James Clear (2005)
- *Change Makers: Make Your Mark with More Impact and Less Drama.* Digby Scott (2019)
- *Doing it Differently: Life and Work After 50.* Geoff Pearman (2016)
- *Finding FISH in a Strengths-Based Practice: Fulfilment, Inspiration,*

Success, and Happiness in a Life Well-Lived, Christopher Miller (2024)

- *First, Break all the Rules: What the World's Greatest Managers Do Differently,* Marcus Buckingham, Gallup Organization (2016)
- *Flexperts: Getting the best from flex in a world that's ever changing.* Gillian Brookes (2023)
- *The Joy of Finding Fish: A Journey of Fulfilment, Inspiration, Success and Happiness.* Christopher Miller (2022)
- *Start with Why: How Great Leaders Inspire Everyone to Take Action.* Simon Sinek (2009)
- *Strengths Based Leadership: Great Leaders, Teams, and Why People Follow.* Tom Rath, Barry Conchie, Gallup organization (2009)
- *Surrounded by Idiots: The Four Types of Human Behaviour (or, How to Understand Those Who Cannot Be Understood).* Thomas Erikson (2019)

ENDNOTES

1   https://www.priyaparker.com/book-art-of-gathering

2   https://maoridictionary.co.nz/word/152

3   https://antoniamilkop.com/2021/09/02/what-is-cliftonstrengths/

4   https://antoniamilkop.com/2022/07/29/team-strengths-dna

5   https://newsroom.heart.org/news/new-survey-91-of-parents-say-their-fam-ily-is-less-stressed-when-they-eat-together

    https://parentingplace.nz/resources/food-for-thought-why-mealtimes-matter

    https://www.gse.harvard.edu/ideas/edcast/20/04/benefit-family-mealtime

6   New Zealand's Social Wellbeing Agency carried out some research via the Families Commission in 2011, which showed that 35% of young people shared meals with their families frequently (7+ times a week); and another 40% shared regular mealtimes (3-6 times per week). However, nearly a quarter remaining quarter (25%) of young people in NZ were either infrequently or never sharing family meals together. https://thehub.swa.govt.nz/assets/documents/RF-eating-together-final.pdf

7   https://www.gallup.com/cliftonstrengths/en/278225/how-to-improve-teamwork.aspx

8   Did you know that managers account for 70% of the variance in employee engagement? Source: Gallup. https://news.gallup.com/businessjour-nal/182792/managers-account-variance-employee-engagement.aspx

9   slido.com, mentimeter.com, miro.com

10 https://www.gallup.com/cliftonstrengths

11 Tuckman, B.W. Developmental sequence in small groups. Psychological Bulletin, 1965, 63(6), 384-399.

12 https://www.scottgraffius.com/blog/files/team-21.html

13 Gallup's CliftonStrengths® talents online assessment: https://www.gallup.com/cliftonstrengths

14 Simon Sinek https://simonsinek.com/golden-circle/

15   https://youtu.be/u4ZoJKF_VuA?si=ihckzIOnmpsJcUag

16   https://www.digbyscott.com/work-with-digby/change-makers

17   https://christophermiller.co.nz

QUOTE SOURCES

Blake Mycoskie: https://quotefancy.com/blake-mycoskie-quotes

Jason Fried: https://www.brainyquote.com/quotes/jason_fried_799331

Ella Fitzgerald & Louis Armstrong:
https://www.youtube.com/watch?v=J2oEmPP5dTM

Patrick Lencioni: Quoted from *The Five Dysfunctions of Teams*

Gallup: Coaching Strengths: Accelerated Strengths Coaching. Gallup®
Strengths.

Henry Ford: https://www.goodreads.com/quotes/118854-coming-together-is-the-beginning-keeping-together-is-progress-working

Dieter Rams: https://www.brainyquote.com/quotes/dieter_rams_174975

Steven Covey: Adapted from the quote "Start with the end in mind" in *The 7 Habits of Highly Effective People* (1989)

Benjamin Franklin: https://www.forbes.com/quotes/1107/

Māori proverb (1): https://natlib.govt.nz/records/22703273

Tony Robbins: https://www.tonyrobbins.com/career-business/where-focus-goes-energy-flows/

Donald Clifton: https://www.gallup.com/cliftonstrengths/en/249602/learning-cliftonstrengths-don-clifton.aspx

John Maxwell: *Teamwork Makes the Dreamwork* (2002)

African Proverb: https://www.amazon.com.au/Want-Alone-Together-African-Proverb/dp/171997084X

Dr. Seuss: *Oh, the Thinks You Can Think!* (1975)

References

Thomas Carlyle: https://www.forbes.com/quotes/9086/

Simon Sinek: https://simonsinek.com/golden-circle/

Jonathan Swift: https://www.brainyquote.com/quotes/jonathan_swift_122246

Leonardo da Vinci: https://www.azquotes.com/quote/303076

Brené Brown: https://brenebrown.com/

Mattie Stepanek: https://www.brainyquote.com/quotes/mattie_stepanek_319300

Māori proverb (2): https://www.rnz.co.nz/national/programmes/morningreport/audio/2018662501/ka-mua-ka-muri-walking-backwards-into-the-future

Julia Child: https://www.goodreads.com/quotes/412272-no-one-is-born-a-great-cook-one-learns-by

About the Author

How can I be a catalyst to ignite potential in others?

ANTONIA'S STORY

Where I'm from

I live in Wellington, New Zealand, often called the world's coolest little capital. Originally from the UK, I moved here in 2004, intending to stay for just a couple of years. However, I fell in love with the country, its people, the outdoors, and my husband. We married in 2009 and have two wonderful children, now 11 and 12 (at the time of writing this). Though far from my original home, New Zealand is truly one of the best places I've ever lived.

The opportunity of 2023

In 2023, my family and I relocated to a village north of Lyon, France, fulfilling our dream of experiencing French life and culture and living closer to our European family for a bit, as well as immersing ourselves in the culture and rich experiences that Europe has to offer, bringing new perspectives to our lives.

We had long dreamed of such an adventure, and after the global pandemic had disrupted our plans of any international travel for a few years, we seized the opportunity to move overseas and make the most of life while our kids were still young. Otherwise, we may have always regretted not living an adventure we'd always dreamed of.

My 'usefulness to the world' during this time away from home was to capture all the useful ingredients and materials from my own experience of facilitating team gatherings and bring them together in a practical book to benefit others. France is a nation of food-passionate people and you may notice a lot of the food-obsession rubbed off on me whilst writing this book! I was gifted the time and space to do so during the year away, and a lot of delicious French food for fuel. I'm incredibly grateful for this opportunity.

What's my why?

In 2019, thanks to an amazing programme I was part of (and still am), Digby Scott's Change Makers,[16] I discovered my life's big question: *'How can I be a catalyst to ignite potential in others so they have more positive impact in their work and life?'* This realisation led me to establish my coaching and facilitation practice after two decades of working in various roles in the public sector.

I worked with a business coach (Christopher Miller[17]) who supported me to help set up my practice. During one of our coaching sessions, Christopher asked me a very powerful question: *"Antonia, over the rest of your career, do you think you will have more impact leading a handful of programmes you really believe in; or would you have more impact coaching the leaders of these programmes?"* That question certainly made me think long and hard about what I was doing with my time and energy. I eventually decided to leave my job in the public sector and fully focus my time on coaching others and facilitating team gatherings. I haven't looked back.

I believe we all benefit from having a big 'why' to lean into and help fuel what we do. Mine has evolved over time and its current version is: *How can I inspire and connect people to unlock their creative potential and work together to make a positive difference?* This book is one of the many outputs that leans into this why.

My journey into professional coaching

I began by coaching more and more individuals in my workplaces. Over time, I discovered a passion for coaching and mentoring others to help them unlock their potential.

In 2018, I became a Gallup-Certified Strengths Coach. This process was a huge turning point in igniting my strengths and catalysing my future career direction. I witnessed the impact that strengths coaching had on other people – just by them becoming aware of their strengths it had a positive impact on their wellbeing, engagement, and performance at work. It was a space where I felt I was really making a difference. I continued to invest in building my coaching skills over time and in 2024, I earned my Professional Certified Coach (PCC) accreditation with the International Coaching Federation (ICF).

Through coaching, particularly in partnering with leaders and managers of teams, I've been able to give so much of what I think is missing in this world –spaces for deep listening, understanding, compassion, non-judgement, and thoughtful questioning. By offering these trusted spaces, individuals have accessed more creative thinking, applying it to problem-solving in ways that are both effective and empowering.

My journey into facilitation

My passion and energy for facilitation came with a slower burn. If someone had told me ten years ago that I'd be an expert facilitator earning a good income through facilitating team gatherings, I'd have laughed in their face! I used to find standing in front of a room of people daunting. However, I loved the challenge of organising purposeful team workshops.

Through training and experience, I gained self-awareness of my strengths as a facilitator and got comfortable with the idea of what facilitation really means – being able to make a process easier for others, leading a group with curiosity and asking questions to help them discover, helping extract their brilliance, and working on bringing out the strengths of a group.

The role of a facilitator is not to be the subject-matter expert in the room, but the person who can create that safe environment and make it easier for participants to engage. Once I changed my mindset around the actual purpose of facilitation, it became a lot more fun. Facilitation is a method of delivery that I've been able to give my joy and energy to.

What I'm hoping this book inspires in you

The desire for writing this book is my way to take all that I've learned and experienced over the years and share this with others – in a form that's digestible, practical, and equips others to become masterful in the way they facilitate their own team gatherings.

If just some of the magic and content in this book inspires you to become more creative with the way your teams spend time together, and that makes a positive difference in what you achieve as a team, then my purpose in this universe is fulfilled!